Introduction

Assessment has subtly undergone significant transformation over the last ten years. Methodologies such as Assessment for Learning or programmes such as the Improving Schools Programme have all had, as their principal goal, the aim of raising children's standards through meaningful dialogue.

Indeed, if assessment could be described in one word it would be that it is a conversation. This conversation takes many forms but essentially revolves around a triad of people: children, parents and professionals. The drive of the conversation stems from a clear understanding of a child's immediate standards, coupled with anticipated attainment. This creates meaningful and personal target-driven learning in which professionals plan according to the needs of the child and the child understands where they need to progress to on their learning journey.

That all sounds very simple but you don't need to be in education very long to know that the simplest plans tend to be the hardest to execute. In order to be able to confidently judge standards, a professional requires three key principles at their fingertips: solid subject knowledge, a good understanding of the child and stable national standards to measure against. Any gaps in these three principles require filling so that judgements can be made with confidence.

Filling these gaps may be just as case of getting to know your class, which is an ongoing process, although generally by October half-term you will have a solid understanding of how they function individually and as a group. Tailoring assessments to each child requires greater sophistication. We are gradually moving away from formal assessments as the core method for collecting evidence and beginning to embrace individualised learning that better reflects the *Every Child Matters* agenda.

Schools are now adopting assessment for learning rather than assessment of learning. This change of direction moves assessment away from being an historic snapshot of ability to a living policy that can actively drive a child's learning.

Uniquely, this book looks at four key assessment programmes in Primary and Early Years education. The aim of the book is to offer sound advice about Assessing Pupils' Progress (APP), the Improving Schools Programme (ISP), Foundation Stage Profiles (FSP) and Assessment for Learning (AfL), whilst drawing out general principles that transcend assessment.

If, as stated, assessment is a conversation, then the best way to start is by talking.

You Can... **Know why we assess**

In recent years there has been a lot of talk about changing the way we measure pupil progress. This raises a number of important questions. Firstly, what do we mean by pupil progress? Is it ongoing, a snapshot review or an holistic examination of the whole child? Secondly, what sort of assessments should we doing? Should we be undertaking summative, evaluative, formative, ongoing or observational assessments? Finally, who does this work? In short, it is a blended mix but how that mix is made depends on the child, the school and your professional experience.

Thinking points

● Assessment is, at heart, the driver for improving learning. For most of the children in your class, it is likely that you can impose the same assessment strategy on them, but for a small group you should consider the appropriateness of the strategy you are using.

● As with learning, there is no one-size-fits-all approach and teachers should apply an intelligent lens on the various programmes or models they can use. If the standard strategy is more intimidating than developmental for a child (as formal tests can be), then don't use it. It will not produce a valid assessment and, importantly, will not be giving that child the best chance. Talking to your assessment leader might offer support for alternative strategies. Typically, children who are at the extremes of learning – the very able and those with learning needs – may require alternative assessment strategies.

Tips, ideas and activities

● Knowing the systems used in your school is the best start. Assessment must have cohesive systems for it to be meaningful, and must have a direct influence on children's learning and how you plan.

● New systems will require professional development (either internally or externally) and time to use them. The longer you use a specific system or programme, the better you will get to know it and the more useful the resulting data will be.

● Understanding your subject is as important as knowing how to perform any assessments. If there is an aspect of the curriculum (particularly the core curriculum) that you feel requires professional development, then speak to a relevant curriculum leader for advice or direction.

● Assessment is a cycle. It starts with an audit of skills, leads to tailored planning, moves to an assessment, moves to targets that are shared with relevant groups (pupils, parents, colleagues and senior leadership) and returns to planning influenced by these targets to begin the cycle again.

● Communication is core to assessment. If children do not know why they have been given a target or what the target is, they have little chance of attaining it. Ideally, children should be part of the target-setting procedure – they are a good judge of their own ability and can offer alternative targets once they are used to how the process works.

● Any adult working in your room should know what assessment processes are taking place and be able to administer them (whether it is an observational or formal assessment). Shared professional development and shared communication will support this process.

YOU CAN

ASSESS PUPILS'
progre~~ss~~

Anthony David

**FOR AGES
4-11**

"....schools which have robust
tracking systems in place achieve
the best rates of progress..."
Sue Hackman Chief Adviser on School Standards

Acknowledgements

Author
Anthony David

Editor
Liz Miles

Development Editor
Niamh O'Carroll

Project Editor
Fabia Lewis

Series Designer
Catherine Perera

Cover Designer
Helen Taylor

Cover photography
Rubberball © 2006

Design
Q2A Media

Text © 2009, Anthony David
© 2009 Scholastic Ltd

Designed using Adobe InDesign

Published by Scholastic Ltd
Villiers House
Clarendon Avenue
Leamington Spa
Warwickshire CV32 5PR

www.scholastic.co.uk

Printed by Bell and Bain Ltd.
1 2 3 4 5 6 7 8 9   9 0 1 2 3 4 5 6 7 8

© Crown copyright and other materials reproduced under the terms of the Click Use Licence.

British Library Cataloguing-in-Publication Data
A catalogue record for this book is available from the British Library.
ISBN 978-1407-10196-5

Mixed Sources
Product group from well-managed forests and other controlled sources
www.fsc.org Cert no. TT-COC-002769
© 1996 Forest Stewardship Council
FSC

Contents

Contents

You Can... Understand the principles of assessing children

If assessment had one clear purpose then it would be a relatively routine task to undertake. But it does not. It has many roles and as a result there are numerous ways of assessing children, hence the need for ongoing, planned, directed and accumulative or test-based assessment – to name a few examples. All these assessment types are directed towards building as complete a picture of the child as possible so that their learning experience is tailored to their identified needs.

Thinking points

● Assessment is, ultimately, a form of communication. Knowing whom you are communicating with and in what form will affect how you present the outcomes of your assessment. Generally there will be three core groups: the children, their parents or carers, and your colleagues. Each group will receive a refined version of your results and not all will share the complete understanding that you have. In having a wide range of assessment styles, you will be able to tailor your assessment meetings (such as pupil conferences, parent consultations or colleague meetings) to the audience.

● Assessment is ongoing – things will just happen in class. Always have an eye open so that you can capture those 'magic moments'. This style of 'ongoing observation' is well established within the Foundation Stage, and is discussed in Chapter 6 of this book.

Tips, ideas and activities

● The children's previous teacher will have a wealth of information, having taught them for the last twelve months. It is likely that your school will have an agreed handover timetable, generally in July. It is worth agreeing at the meeting that, in September, you can review your colleague's assessments once you have got to know the new class, so that any variances with your initial observations can be identified and reviewed.

● Plan for a range of assessments. Typically, formal assessments, such as test-based assessments, will occur at set times during the year (traditionally in October, February and May, to monitor progress). However, this only gives a snapshot of how well a child is attaining on one given day rather than reflecting their whole ability (they may have had an off day or simply not respond well under test conditions). A range of assessment styles, such as observational, photographic, video or oral, will give a more complete picture.

● As with a learning objective, aim to keep your assessment focus as clear and defined as possible. The Assessing Pupils' Progress (APP) programme, launched by the DCSF in 2008, has refined the learning objectives set out in the renewed Frameworks for literacy and maths to support these core areas of learning (see Chapter 2) and will help you to make your assessment objectives accurate.

● Children need to know what it is you are assessing and how you are going to do it. If it is how well they can sing and that you will be recording for assessment purposes, then tell them.

● Be clear yourself about the purpose of your assessment and how it will be levelled. How you assess history will be different to how you assess literacy, and understanding the purposes of each will support your planning.

You Can... **Understand the different types of assessment**

Different assessment styles meet different needs. Understanding how these styles work supports planning and ensures greater accuracy in your assessment outcomes. Ultimately, you are aiming to create a picture of the whole child and this is done through end-of-year reports, formative tracking during the year and ongoing accumulative assessment through observation. A balanced approach using a combination of these styles supports the process of understanding the whole child, therefore allowing you to plan their learning opportunities based on your assessment conclusions.

Thinking points

● A Learning Contract can be a useful way of creating an achievable target for a child or group of children. Typically, a Learning Contract will: diagnose the learning needs, identify the appropriate learning objectives (and the resources required to deliver those objectives), set a reasonable time limit, and communicate expectations to the learners. The contracts do not need to be lengthy and will often be a natural extension of existing targets (such as the 'I can' statements used in many schools). Keep the contract specific, and highlight lessons in which the targets will be taught.

● Common errors in assessment often appear in formative tests, which are generally published by an external company. If you have children who are new to English you should be aware of the wording used and equally, if a child can access the language but is new to the country you should check for unknown cultural references.

Tips, ideas and activities

● The role of IT is growing. It offers ease of access, along with the ability to quickly scrutinise results and to create meaningful data. Chapter 7 goes into greater detail but, in summary, all the forms of assessment listed below can now be accessed in some way through IT. Understanding what is available can potentially sharpen and speed up your assessments. A word of caution: don't let the IT lead the assessment – it is your responsibility to understand how you can make it work for you.

● In recent years, formative test-based assessments have had most publicity in the form of end-of-key-stage tests, known as SATs (the name was dropped in the early 1990s but has stayed in common circulation). This form of assessment – be it a weekly spelling test or end-of-year paper – gives a snapshot of performance, based on building towards a known date.

● Ongoing accumulative assessment is where information is collected as part of an ongoing procedure. Commonly used in the Foundation Stage, it is now reaching up into higher years in many schools as it potentially provides a broader picture of the child. Assessment under these conditions tends to be less intense.

● Summative assessments are a review of a child's ability. Typically within schools, this takes the form of a written end-of-year report as the most detailed summative assessment. This document, as the only formal piece of evidence presented to parents, traditionally holds great status by all and the temptation by many teachers is to fill it with professional language. Generally, this will go over the heads of most parents, who might then fail to understand this important document. The style of language should always be simple, allowing your assessments to speak for themselves.

You Can... Explain the importance of assessment to your families

As a general rule, the people that children want to impress the most is not the teacher, as we would like it, but their parents, and increasingly parents are being referred to as 'home-teachers'. Involving parents in your assessment conversations will empower them to be that crucial home link that takes theoretical learning into the real world. Many everyday experiences, such as shopping and reading the paper, are not possible in the classroom and have greater meaning outside school. Involving parents in the assessment process will give them the necessary authority at home to direct out-of-school learning.

Thinking points

● There are a lot of tutor agencies that have grown as cottage industries in the last few years, with the development of the internet. As any tutors used are part of the child's learning circle it is important that school-based assessments are shared with them. It is another dialogue and in this case it is the parents'/carers' responsibility to exchange assessment outcomes between yourself and the tutor. Identify whether a child has a tutor as soon as possible so that you can share assessment outcomes. It is useful if you can add this to your first parent consultation in the autumn term.

● Parent consultations are an invaluable part of the school year. Regrettably, many parents find this meeting difficult, often because of negative preconceived ideas. Although it sounds obvious, a warm smile at the start of the meeting can set a good tone.

Tips, ideas and activities

● Target setting is now used in most schools (a range of target-setting models is described on page 10). As teacher, your role is to support parents in unpicking what the assessment targets are and what needs to be done to achieve the goals. Equally, Ofsted now ask children: a) What is your target? and b) What do you need to do in order to achieve it? If you are clear in your mind about how to do this and have shared it with the parent/carer this increases the chances of a child's exposure to appropriate learning opportunities.

● Be careful not to use too many acronyms or jargon when talking to parents. However well informed the parent or carer may be, the teaching profession is littered with terminology that most professionals can barely keep up with. If you do have to use acronyms, such as SEN (Special Educational Needs), then explain what the acronym means and ensure you use it in an appropriate context.

● Using translators is now commonplace in most urban schools, reflecting the multicultural intake of children. There are extreme examples (some London boroughs boast over a hundred different nationalities) but generally one or two languages will dominate. Arranging a translation service not only demonstrates a school's commitment to that family but ensures that assessments are understood when shared. Also knowing who speaks the community language within your school can prove to be invaluable if you need to talk to a parent quickly.

● Be sensitive when timing your conversation. If you have a genuine concern, then it is appropriate to agree a meeting with the parents rather than to bring it up in conversation in the playground. It is reasonable to briefly explain why you would like to see them, and professional to assume that your conversation will not be held in public.

You Can... Help children notice their assessment targets

Setting targets for pupils puts standards at the heart of their learning. It helps children identify what they need to do in order to improve. Targets also support teachers when planning future learning. For this process to be successful, the child will need to both know what the target requires and how to achieve it. Therefore, the role of the teacher is to ensure that children clearly understand their targets and when those targets are being taught.

Thinking points

There is a role for a single whole-school target, sometimes referred to as learning journeys or learning ladders. In either case a core target is highlighted from each year group and written as a ladder or on a pathway. The advantage of a pathway (see 'Learning journey' photocopiable, page 60) is that the learning movement is linear rather than hierarchical. When creating these core targets (six in total across a typical primary school), it is important to identify what a child needs to do in order to achieve the target. In essence you create three sub-targets per target. A whole-school approach such as this demonstrates progression across the years. When selecting an area of learning, such as problem solving, ensure that you all use the same learning focus, allowing the targets to track clearly across year groups.

Tips, ideas and activities

- When writing a target, keep the language simple and clear.

- Highlight what children need to do in order to achieve the target.

- A child must clearly know what their targets are if they are to maximise their chances of meeting them. Arrange a five-minute pupil conference once every half-term with yourself or your teaching assistant to give you a reasonable amount of time to discuss the current targets and examine progression. Although potentially time-consuming, pupil conferences can form part of your weekly timetable in much the same way as other regular groups do, such as reading groups. The child will value this one-to-one attention and keep their targets fresh in their mind.

- Setting group targets is a useful way of organising your planning and grouping by ability. Group targets can be reviewed weekly as you rotate your teaching time across the class. Although there are many time pressures, it is good practice to quickly remind the group of what their targets are and what it is they need to do in order to meet them. This will need around 20 minutes to discuss when you present new targets each term/half-term but only quick reminders afterwards.

- Setting children, particularly for maths, has become increasingly popular and is an efficient way of grouping by ability. Theoretically, a teacher is able to fine-tune their planning to meet the learning needs of the children within the set. However, children in lower sets lose the active examples of more able learners. Although setting is a useful way of deploying resources, it should be approached with caution and should not be exclusively done all week – there should be opportunities for the class to learn together.

You Can... Write personalised, parent-friendly annual reports

End-of-year reports are the culmination of a range of assessments and, in many cases, the last learning conversation you have with your current parents. They are an opportunity to reflect on how well the child has developed academically as well as how they have grown as an individual. Capturing the essence of an individual child in less than two pages is a challenge. If you are new to report writing it is worth speaking to your headteacher and asking to read the reports of any colleagues who are good at writing them.

Thinking points

● Before you actually start writing a report, ask yourself what you know of the child: What challenges has this child overcome? How have they grown? What areas do they need to develop? What targets do they need to address?

● Report-writing programs can save hours of time. However, a cut-and-paste approach to report writing can produce something that lacks personality (both the child's and yours) or, at worst, a report that does not reflect the child. If your school is investing in a program it is useful to find out if final reports can be 'tweaked' so that you can put the personality back in.

● You should be bringing together your assessment material in April/May and begin writing your reports in May for a completion date in mid-June, so they are ready to send out in early July.

Tips, ideas and activities

● Avoid jargon and acronyms. Reports should be straightforward but informative. Your parents/carers will want to support their children's learning, and reports full of jargon will make it difficult for them to understand how they can do this. Equally, a parent/carer might have had a difficult experience while at school themselves and although jargon sounds professional, it might reinforce their experience.

● Take care when writing about maths. In this country, it is almost fashionable to say we are bad at the subject, so a sensitive report can present a positive image of the subject.

● Talk about the child. It is a simple thing to say, but when faced with over a dozen subjects to write about, the character of the child can get lost in cut-and-paste comments.

● Use a clear font to write with, such as Arial, Helvetica or Gill Sans. Comic Sans is not necessarily appropriate for a professional document. Also, use a font size between 10 and 12 points. Any smaller is hard to read and any larger looks as if you are filling space.

● Certain aspects of a report can be written during the year, such as on specific projects or trips. Spreading the workload can make the process easier.

● Always re-read a report after you have finished it. Ideally, print a copy, as errors are always easier to spot on paper than on the screen (such as the ubiquitous wrong name or gender).

● If you have a willing partner or friend, ask them to read a selection of final reports for an opinion on how well they read.

● If English is not the first language for some of your parents you will need to take into consideration additional time for translation services.

You Can... **Learn more about assessment from other authors**

Two core principles behind learning are to understand what a learner already knows and to understand that we must assess. It should be of little surprise, then, that assessment has been an aspect of education that has been written and rewritten about many times. And when a subject has been written about extensively certain champions arise. Below is a list of a few of the finest assessment contributors. Between them they have written nearly a hundred books on the subject, but if you read just one you will be better off!

Thinking points

In the last five years three major assessment programmes have been developed: Assessment for Learning (AfL), the Improving Schools Programme (ISP) and Assessing Pupils' Progress (APP). Almost all the material is available exclusively online. The advantage of this online material is that it is available to read immediately. However, it must be found and you need to know how. Your local authority consultants should keep you informed of any changes or titles that will be of interest. You should also apply a personal filter when using an internet search as some of the material you come across may be aimed at a different audience.

Tips, ideas and activities

● Shirley Clarke is one of the country's leading experts on practical, formative ways to assess children. Forerunners of Assessment for Learning, her books are packed with practical tips and ideas on how to get the most from assessment opportunities. Her background was founded in primary education, from which she moved on to work as a primary maths consultant, followed by a decade as a lecturer at the Institute of Education. She now spends her time as an independent consultant in both the UK and the USA. All details of her courses and books can be found at www.shirleyclarke-education.org.

● Before his death in November 2005, Ted Wragg was one of the country's great commentators on education. Barely a subject missed his pragmatic and witty attention in his regular columns for the *TES* and the *Guardian's* education supplement. At the time of his death he had written over 50 books and, although their subject matter varied, assessment was often at the heart of them. Each book is tightly written and full of gems.

● Angela Woodfield brings a great deal of experience to her writing. She is one of the authors of *Assessment for Learning and Teaching in Primary Schools*, which is a clear introduction to the different kinds of assessment and their purposes for new teachers.

● If you are printing an online document on assessment, set your printer to black and white, as any photographs will use a lot of coloured ink. Check how many pages need printing. More than 15 to 20 pages will be difficult to store as a loose document. Also consider if it is necessary to print at all. Although a document is easier to read when printed, it is a waste of ink/paper if you are not going to use the document again. Your school may have a policy of re-using printed paper.

You Can... Utilise other adults in your classroom when assessing

In the last five years a virtual army of Teaching Assistants (TAs) have been recruited into primary schools across the country. Their use within schools varies depending on the need of the establishment but what has significantly changed is their profile. Gone are the days when TAs did the photocopying or display mounting. Today, a TA's core purpose is teaching and being a co-teacher within the classroom. This has resulted in their improved professional development, performance management and raised expectations, for example in being an active partner in the assessment process.

Thinking points
● Everyone who works in a school has a part to play in raising standards and giving pupils a better start in life. As a result everyone should expect to receive appropriate professional development from the time they start working. Introductory training helps new TAs and support staff to understand their role, feel confident in their work and be effective members of the school team. Longer-serving staff will also find it useful as a refresher to bring them up to date with policies and practice. Involving your TAs in your Continuing Professional Development (CPD) programmes alongside teachers will ensure that all the adults in your classrooms are aware of current practice and work towards a common purpose.

● Increasingly, specialist TAs and Higher Level Teaching Assistants (HLTAs) are becoming responsible for aspects of school life. Appropriate assessment training should be part of their training if they are to take on new areas of leadership.

Tips, ideas and activities
● Consider your communication with the TAs in your class. What strategies have you in place so that they know what you are intending to teach and how you intend to differentiate? Communication is key and you will find a suggested communication sheet on page 57. Your TA should be fully involved with the learning and assessment cycle. Key to this is how you both manage to discuss observations from the pupils' behaviour.

● If possible, involve your TA in part or all of your planning sessions (during PPA time), so that they have an overall view of the short-term plans.

● How do you deploy the TAs within your school? There are many models, including class-share TAs, specialised TAs and TAs who are allocated to specific children. Understanding this model will support any decisions you consider that have a school-wide impact, such as professional development or structural changes, and could have an impact on how you plan your assessment opportunities.

● Assessment opportunities can be hard to write down when you are involved with a group. Using a TA to observe (or the other way round) can capture valuable moments.

● Your TA can be a time saver. If you are intending to assess large sections of the class, well-planned work can allow you to split the assessments between you.

● How are the TAs utilised within your school for your subject? It may be that one of your TAs has a particular skill, such as sports or music. It is possible to regrade a TA to include a specialism within their job description, equivalent to a teacher's teaching and learning responsibility (TLR) point.

You Can... Assess children who have English as another language

Assessing the standards of children who do not have English as their dominant language is challenging. While learners with English as an additional language share many characteristics with those whose first language is English, they also have distinctive needs that differ from those of other learners. A typically English-based assessment will not take aptitude into consideration. Maths, for example, is generally considered a universal language but solving maths problems may require support so that the child is able to sift the maths out of the language. Knowing the level of language acquisition is an essential filter before applying assessment results.

Thinking points

● Understanding how well a child communicates in their home language can provide evidence to support learning plateaus. Assessing a home language requires specialised support but can be useful when developing school targets. It can also be a way of involving parents, particularly if they speak little English themselves.

● Presenting positive role models is an important piece of work that does not necessarily have to take place at set times, such as in October during Black History Month. It should be ongoing and identified when opportunities present themselves, such as when President Obama was inaugurated in January 2009.

● Schools can capitalise on the new emphasis on modern foreign languages. They are no longer institutes where English is the only language. A blend of languages and cultures can potentially bring exciting opportunities to the school. Schools must consider how they can reach out to groups in order to make them feel part of the community.

Tips, ideas and activities

● Tracking language acquisition expectations is as important as any other form of tracking. The same principles apply: look for plateaus; is the child progressing as expected? what barriers are preventing them from progressing beyond their current level of acquisition?

● Hilary Hester has written a number of books on the stages of English learning and is a recognised expert in the field. She has developed a four-point scale that focuses on language acquisition alongside social aspects of learning. How a child develops is reliant on the individual child, the support provided by the school and the school's environment:

- Stage 1 reflects initial interaction, joining in but not necessarily speaking when the child is new to the language.
- Stage 2 is when a child is becoming familiar with the language and is able to hold conversations with peers but relies on support for more complex communication.
- Stage 3 is when a child is becoming more confident with the language and understands idioms such as puns and metaphors.
- Stage 4 is a child who is a very fluent user of the language.

● Children should be assessed for stages of language acquisition at least twice a year. Ongoing daily observations and targets can also support development.

● Providing support as soon as is practical can prevent secondary behaviours developing in a child who may be feeling frustrated because they cannot communicate at the level they expect. More importantly, support reflects a commitment to the principle that every child matters. An Ethnic Minority Achievement (EMA) team – either within your school or centrally – should be able to provide support or advice.

You Can... Understand the 10 basic principles of Assessment for Learning

The principles behind Assessment for Learning (AfL) are that learners will improve most when they understand their learning objectives, where they need to progress to and what they need to do in order to get there. As with any assessment process, the core aim of AfL is to raise pupils' achievement. How it differs from other strategies is in the direct engagement of the learner with their learning. This dialogue has proved to be a powerful way of raising achievement for individuals and across whole schools.

Thinking points

● The Assessment Reform Group (ARG) was created in 1996 (previously known as the Policy Task Group on Assessment) with the core aim of ensuring that assessment policy and practice at all levels takes into account relevant research and development. Since then, it has refined policy practice on AfL with the underlying principle that 'Assessment for Learning is the process of seeking and interpreting evidence for use by learners and their teachers to decide where the learners are in their learning, where they need to go and how best to get there.' (*Assessment for Learning: 10 Principles*, ARG 2002)

● Supporting all the principles of AfL means involving your community. This includes directing learners' accountability to their learning which, by default, will involve their parents, colleagues and the children themselves.

Tips, ideas and activities

● Ten core principles underpin AfL. The principles of AfL state that:

- It should be part of effective planning of teaching and learning.
- It should focus on how students learn.
- It should be recognised as central to classroom practice.
- It should be regarded as a key professional skill for teachers.
- It should be sensitive and constructive.
- It should take account of the importance of learner motivation.
- It should promote commitment to learning goals and a shared understanding of the criteria by which they are assessed.
- Learners should receive constructive guidance about how to improve.
- It develops learners' capacity for self-assessment so that they can become reflective and self-managing.
- It should recognise the full range of achievements of all learners.

● The rest of this chapter will unpick how practitioners can implement these ten principles.

● For more information about AFL visit www.qca.org.uk/qca_4336.aspx

You Can... Know the characteristics of Assessment for Learning

Research has shown that children's standards rise at a steeper rate when they are fully involved in the assessment process. Taking ownership of their learning path is empowering, creating an active participant rather than a passive member of the class. Encouraging children to take an active part in the assessment process and planning opportunities that encourage progression are, arguably, the core characteristics of Assessment for Learning.

Thinking points

- Assessment *for* learning (formative assessment) is different to the assessment *of* learning (summative assessment). This is equivalent to comparing ongoing assessment with end-of-unit tests that are rated against National Standards. Summative assessment is important as part of a school's understanding of progression but does not allow for an ongoing refinement of skills. Equally, it does not give the learner the opportunity to set challenging targets, whether these have been agreed or self-imposed, which removes the sense of success when a target has been met. Assessment *of* Learning reflects a learner's past whereas Assessment *for* Learning is current and future-driven.

- AfL skills are transferable. When reference is made to the 'learner', it could refer to the pupil or an adult. Taking ownership of assessment needs, supported by a culture that is determined by success, is arguably good practice in any establishment.

Tips, ideas and activities

- To effectively use AfL you need to know your class well. Given that most primary classes change teacher each year it is important that your meetings with the previous teacher cover assessment, characteristics and matters of significant importance for each child. You should maintain a dialogue with the previous teacher for at least the first half-term.

- Continually raise the profile of learning objectives. Using child-friendly language, highlight them several times during a lesson, including the plenary.

- Build time into your weekly timetable for individual reviews or target setting with some of the children.

- Show children's work that has met the criteria. This can be done at any point during the lesson.

- Lesson plans should show clear evidence that AfL opportunities are being planned for. These could be discrete targets for small groups or individuals, or whole-class targets formed round the types of questioning or objective being taught.

- The Assessment Reform Group identified seven key characteristics of AfL (Assessment Reform Group, 1999, *Assessment for Learning*):
  - It is embedded in a view of teaching and learning of which it is an essential part.
  - It involves sharing learning goals with learners.
  - It aims to help pupils to know and to recognise the standards for which they are aiming.
  - It involves pupils in self-assessment (and peer assessment).
  - It provides feedback that leads to pupils recognising their next steps and how to take them.
  - It is underpinned by the confidence that every student can improve.
  - It involves both teacher and pupils reviewing and reflecting on assessment data.

You Can... **Use effective questioning**

Effective questioning is central to Assessment for Learning (AfL) as it not only reveals what a child knows but also how they know it. By strategically asking a mix of questions, the teacher is able to identify learning gaps or learning leaps. Open-ended questions are more likely to involve the child within the learning process, making them further accountable for their own learning. Being good at asking questions requires practice but is an invaluable assessment tool that is quick to administer and provides immediate results.

Thinking points

● Plan your questions. They should reflect a range of styles and meet the needs of different abilities within the class. How children answer these questions should reflect your assessment criteria. How you ask a question changes the demands made upon a child in the use of vocabulary, depth of understanding and the thought processes needed for the answer.

● Changing a direct question to one that is broader in approach can offer greater challenge. For example, the question, 'Is 11 a prime number?' can only be answered with 'yes' or 'no'. Asking, 'Why is 11 a prime number?' reveals a child's mathematical knowledge, providing an opportunity for them to model key words (in this case 'prime') and to demonstrate their grasp on the subject.

● A range of question starters includes:

   ● How can we be sure that... ?

   ● What is the same and what is different about... ?

   ● Is it ever/always true/false that... ?

   ● How do you... ?

   ● How would you explain... ?

   ● What does that tell us about... ?

   ● What is wrong with... ?

   ● Why is... true?

Tips, ideas and activities

● Allow longer periods of time for children to answer a question. This gives children space to consider their answer and give more detailed replies.

● Using 'talk partners', where children are invited to discuss the question rather than think about it in isolation, is less stressful than traditional methods and invites less vocal members of the class to share the discussion. Overhearing other conversations also provides an opportunity for children to gather a wider range of opinions than they would if a teacher picked individuals to answer the question. Talking about a subject engages the learner and more effectively reinforces the learning objective than passive listening does.

● Encourage children to answer using the specific vocabulary in the lesson. This will demonstrate that they are able to model the learning objective.

● How you structure your questions will determine the type of answer. A mix of questions, closed and open, will give pace to the lesson.

● Plan your questions but equally pose questions that naturally come from the learning.

● Use questions to find out what children know.

● Avoid trick questions or 'yes' and 'no' answers.

● The learning environment will affect the range of answers; typically, relaxed children will give deeper answers.

● Use questions to identify learning gaps or misunderstandings.

● There will always be a handful of children who want to answer everything. Select a blend of volunteer and non-volunteer answers.

You Can... **Be a smart marker**

Reading and responding to children's work is vital because their writing is the evidence that generally supports whether a learning objective have been understood or not. That said, marking requires purpose. Many colleagues will be aware of the negative impact of over marking, effectively moving the goal posts, and muddling the main purpose with additional expectations. Even if the objective has been met, the learner can be overpowered by additional marking. It's not that common errors are to be ignored; it's simply being honest with the children about your marking intentions. Smart marking can be key to seeing standards improve.

Thinking points

● There will be periods when marking will need to be thorough. Typically, these will fall during assessment weeks. In these cases explain to the class what additional areas you will be expecting to assess in your marking. It is not unreasonable to mark presentation because, although small, it does form part of the marking equation for the end of Key Stage 2 writing papers.

● There are times when it is more important to be systematic in your marking. You may perform diagnostic marking assessments when you have a concern or if a child is new to the class and you want to ascertain prior learning. Using a standard diagnostic test (there are many on the market) is useful but only when the implications identified by the test are followed up within the class in the subsequent lessons. Existing planning will have to be adapted to reflect the diagnosis.

● Styles of language that you can use in your comments include:

   ● Reminder prompt – How do you think… ?

   ● Scaffolded prompt – An order or direction, eg Describe… What do you think… ?

   ● An example prompt – Give two examples.

Tips, ideas and activities

● Keep your marking intentions clear. If a child is learning a new strategy, then mark to that objective. If you are including presentation and common errors in your marking, clearly highlight this early in the lesson.

● Involve children with the marking process. The objectives should be clear enough for a child to identify if a peer has met them. For example, if you are creating similes children should be able to identify if a peer has responded appropriately. This creates a useful second layer of informal assessment (see page 20 for more strategies on how to encourage peer-to-peer marking).

● When marking, identify what has been done well, followed by a next step. This model of affirmation and challenge supports a learner and is less threatening than punitive corrections.

● Aim to follow up marking with oral feedback. Reading a teacher's comments (if the children are able to read them) is a passive act. Oral feedback, however, is the start of a discussion that, arguably, is the most powerful way to raise standards as it sets levels of accountability between learner and teacher. When oral feedback is not possible, encourage written responses to your marking. This requires training and encouragement but is a useful way of engaging learners with your comments.

● Marking should be timely. It has little impact if it is out of date.

● If you are using highlighters when marking, ensure the children understand what the colours refer to and aim to keep to no more than three different colours.

● Use agreed school procedures.

You Can... Involve children as part of the assessment process

Assessment is a dialogue, and perhaps the most important dialogue is between you and the child. How you pitch this conversation will depend on a number of factors: your relationship, their maturity, their ability and how confident they are with the whole process. Involving children with the assessment process (and getting the most from it) will require as much age-appropriate training as you would expect for yourself. But once involved, it is an empowering way for a child to take control of their learning.

Thinking points

● When presented with a new programme or strategy, you would expect professional training. In much the same way, children at an age-appropriate level require similar amounts of training if they are going to get the most from the assessment process. How you train them will depend on the class and might take the form of a whole-class or group explanation. Children should understand why they are assessed. Without fully understanding the purpose of assessment (that it directs your learning so that you can improve your standards), they will not be able to access their full entitlement from education.

● Involving children in their assessment is empowering but does take time. However, it is time well spent. Peer assessment is a time-efficient model but should not be relied on alone. Individual meetings (perhaps termly) not only reinforce assessment targets but also provide a valuable opportunity to build the relationship between yourself and the child.

Tips, ideas and activities

● Use child-friendly language. There has been a tendency in recent years for teachers to overuse professional language and, although there is a time and place for professional terms, if the child does not understand the context you will be talking over their heads.

● Avoid using acronyms. Children are unlikely to know what they mean.

● Let the children know in advance when you are going to talk to them about their targets. It doesn't need to be weeks in advance but a few days will allow them to get ready for you.

● Letting children know what their targets are is only half the story. They need to know how to achieve their targets. When setting targets consider what steps are needed to achieve them. Include these steps with the target as 'steps to success'. Aside from this being a useful way for children to understand how to achieve their target, it is also good preparation for visits from Ofsted who will be asking children what they need to do in order to reach their target.

● Celebrate success. This will enthuse the child and make them feel, rightfully, proud of their achievement. It will also encourage them when presented with the next target.

● If a target has not been reached be honest with the child and try to reset it so that it can be achieved. It is not uncommon at the start of the year, when you are getting to know your class, to set ambitious targets. Equally it might be an area of learning that the child is not yet ready to understand. There are likely to be other occasions during the year when they can try to reach the target, again and sometimes a complete change can give enough space for the child to attempt the target with renewed confidence.

You Can... **Lead peer marking**

If good assessment is a dialogue, then involving children in this dialogue with their peers can only go towards reinforcing learning objectives. There is a certain amount of training required if the children are to have meaningful conversations, but once achieved, peer marking can be a powerful tool in the classroom. When learners understand where they are, what their objective is and how to get there, then standards will rise. The dialogue in peer assessment is another direction from which this understanding can come, encouraging them to become more independent learners.

Thinking points

● The role of the teacher changes when children become regular peer markers and as you move from a direct style of teaching towards becoming a facilitator/ mediator between learners. It is important that you are available to answer higher-level questions but all low- and many medium-level queries will generally be resolved without your intervention. This is, however, dependent on the clarity of your assessment criteria.

● Peer marking is not a quick route to less marking – far from it. It requires you, the lead assessor, to have a clear set of marking criteria, which you expect the children to assess against. The marking can then be fairly moderated. It also requires that you match markers to minimise the need for mediation if disputes arise.

Tips, ideas and activities

● Marking criteria must be clear and supported with model answers so that children have confidence in marking.

● Praise good marking and peer-marking teams. This will reinforce your standards and provide additional examples of expectation.

● Peer marking should not be to used to rank children. Peer groups will tend not to be as challenged if they are matched against ability peers. Generally, children tend to adopt a 'teacher-like' style when marking that can remove peer-barriers. However, it is important to be sensitive.

● Be available to provide rapid feedback to avoid misconceptions and regularly highlight good work.

● Invite feedback from the peer partners to the whole class, particularly from the child whose work was marked. Did they use the correct marking criteria? Did they think their partner's comments were fair? Did they offer any suggestions for next steps? This will help clarify the learning point to the child whose work is being marked and affirm the ability of the child who led the peer marking.

● Peer partners should mark one piece of work at a time, not both.

● Encourage children to mark their own work. This is an important step towards becoming an independent learner.

● There will always be a small minority of children who will not feel satisfied by this method of marking. It is important that you continue in the role of prime assessor for these children.

● Ensure that parents understand what peer marking is and how you use it within the class. They may need assurance that you control how work is assessed and that standards remain.

You Can... Use Assessment for Learning as part of your professional development

An aspect of assessment, whether it is Assessment for Learning (AfL) or another programme, should form part of your professional development. Historically, this would have taken place outside your school at your local Professional Development Centre, giving you the benefits of the big picture from experienced trainers. Increasingly, however, schools are using the wealth of experience and knowledge within their own school to present and lead this subject. Your immediate colleagues will have in-depth knowledge and experience of how to assess and what it should look like.

Thinking points

● Being able to assess meaningfully and for that assessment to have impact on children's learning is a key skill of all teachers. Specifically AfL forms one of the core principles of the Department for Children, Schools and Families (DCSF) as it is central to teaching and learning.

● In as much as teachers need to be able to teach, they must have the appropriate skills needed to interpret the impact their teaching has on their learners. Just as it is reasonable to expect the curriculum to change over time, it is also reasonable to review and adapt the assessment procedures used across your school and in your classroom.

● Parents and carers will expect to be informed of your assessment procedures. Consider your audience and appropriately pitch your language without compromising any core themes. Parents need to be trained as much as colleagues, pupils and yourself.

Tips, ideas and activities

● It is likely that there is one colleague on your team) who is successfully using AfL in their classroom. Not only will they be able to present real-life case studies that involve children and families that you know but they will also be able to digest key AfL points into bite-size chunks. A phase leader or Senior School Leader should be able to direct you to lead professionals.

● Assessment meetings need not be formal and can take place over a cup of coffee or lunch once you have established the key principles in your classroom. This ongoing, casual feedback is not possible with external providers.

● Moderate each other's assessments. A shared time, such as a twilight training session, where phase groups or key stages can meet is ideal. This will allow you time to evaluate your assessment outcomes with colleagues.

● Assessment training should be a regular event within your school's professional development calendar, ideally with some sort of session each half-term. Training and moderation focuses should cover the types of target you set, book-look, planning, and reviewing current pupil assessment trends.

● The National Strategies website contains nationally directed training on AfL. Search for 'AfL CPD' at www.nationalstrategies. standards.dcsf.gov.uk. There is also a regular AfL newsletter on the website that provides case studies, current practice and AfL developments. Search for 'AfL e-bulletin' at the above website.

● Teachers TV (www.teachers.tv) contains thousands of short films that can form part of your own personal development or be used within a training session at school. Search for 'Primary Assessment for Learning' at the website.

You Can... Write learning journeys with your colleagues

Learning targets ('I can' statements) serve a very strategic purpose in shaping the beginning of a child's personal learning journey. But, if targets stand alone they can become long-term outcomes rather than stepping stones of achievement in the ongoing learning process. If we are to prepare today's learners to be learners for life they must understand what part of the learning journey they are on and where it fits into the bigger picture.

Thinking points

Ofsted inspectors have begun to alter how they interview children. Previously they would have been satisfied with a child knowing what their personal target was. Now they expect a child to know what their target is and what they need to do in order to achieve it. This additional level of scrutiny is necessary if the inspector is to be satisfied that the child they are speaking to has a clear understanding of their direction of learning. It is your responsibility to communicate what steps need to be taken so that a target can be achieved and to regularly review it so that a child is able to monitor their learning. Indeed, regardless of whether it's an inspector or another pupil asking, your children should know what they need to do to achieve their current targets and have an awareness of the requirements for future targets.

Tips, ideas and activities

● A learning journey is a metaphorical pathway of linked objectives that stretch from Reception to Year 6 and beyond. Each step on the path is a target (that may have been given in isolation in the past) and each target will be bullet pointed with what a learner needs to understand in order to achieve the target. The Learning Journey pathway (photocopiable, page 60) can be adapted for use in school.

● A single strand will help coordinate the learning journey across the school. For example, it may be an aspect of problem solving in maths or non-narrative fiction in literacy. By focusing on one element or strand, your colleagues will be able to create targets that can be tracked. This will demonstrate progression and support pupils, who will be able to monitor where they are on the learning journey.

● Mapping a learning journey across the school will support parents'/carers' understanding of what needs to be achieved in order to meet the target.

● Targets will need to be refreshed or changed. How often this is done will depend on the school policy and feedback from teachers but typically a target should remain for around a term.

● Introduce new targets at half-term to coincide with parent/carer consultations and allow the end-of-school-year target to straddle the summer holiday into the autumn term.

● Each class should have a set of current targets displayed in their classroom; each child will have his or her own set with an appropriate target highlighted and shared with parents.

● Display an enlarged set of targets within the school. During the term add pieces of work that show the steps needed to achieve a target and indicate progression in learning for a particular theme/focus.

You Can... **Give pupils a voice**

Children are the prime 'clients' within a school and as with any institution they will only get out of it what they are willing to put in. Research by the Assessment Research Group (ARG) and Consulting Pupils on the Assessment of their Learning (CPAL) both concluded that when children actively take part in the assessment process they become more committed to their schooling. The knock-on effect is that the child is happier within the learning environment, and this has a positive impact on their outcomes.

Thinking points

● In 2003 Professor Jean Rudduck and her team at the University of Cambridge conducted research on pupil involvement in assessment. The team concluded that when pupils were actively involved in the assessment process they were more committed to their schooling, it improved pupil self-esteem and transformed the teacher-pupil relationship ('from passive or oppositional to more active and collaborative'). (*Consulting Pupils about Teaching and Learning*, J Rudduck, M Arno, M Fielding, D McIntyre & J Flutter, 2003)

● Adopting this type of policy can have its drawbacks. It may lead to additional marking, noisier classrooms and restrictions on time. Nevertheless, adopting an AfL philosophy has the power to positively alter the pupil-teacher relationship. This balancing of power can be one of the building blocks in creating a climate of increased trust in the classroom.

Tips, ideas and activities

● Dedicate time for this activity. You may well have timetabled sessions for reading, handwriting or lower-level tasks, which are good times to meet with a group or individual to discuss their targets.

● Evaluating goals is an ongoing process. The review, once the goals/targets have been set, should form part of a weekly conversation. How you fit this into your weekly routine will depend on your timetable but, as an example, it could be done when reading with a child/group – take a couple of minutes at the end of the activity to review targets and assess progress.

● Invite children to assess their own work. Page 20 gives suggestions on peer marking which is the beginning of allowing a child to be able to self-evaluate his or her progress. This type of assessment requires a certain level of sophistication and some of the early self-assessments will vary in depth of understanding. However, this skill improves with more opportunities. Whether you do this type of assessment through individual pupil conferences or with peers, it should be planned for in the same way as you plan for questioning.

● Keep the wording for any targets clear and concise. Ideally, the target should be written in consultation with the child so that they fully understand why it has been set.

● Value what a child says. This does not mean they should not be challenged, but actively seeking pupils' comments (rather than imposing your thoughts, however well-intentioned they may be) implies you are going to listen to what they have to say.

● Carefully consider your success criteria for a lesson. Children, particularly those who have special educational needs, should be able to judge their work more accurately if they clearly understand what it is you are expecting them to do.

You Can... **Understand the Single Plan**

Assessment for Learning (AfL) is a significant step towards addressing the Every Child Matters *agenda, as it focuses assessment and improvement on the individual child through a range of complementary interventions. A wide range of key professionals who have an interest in every child's attainment leads these. From this the government developed a new scheme called the New Relationship with Schools (NRwS) that significantly ties* Every Child Matters *to assessment. This is done through the use of a Single Plan for children and schools and builds on the work established by AfL intervention.*

Thinking points

David Miliband launched New Relationships with Schools (NRwS) at the North of England Education Conference, 8 January 2004. During his speech he laid out his ideas of what assessment and individualised learning should look like:

'Decisive progress in educational standards occurs where every child matters; careful attention is paid to their individual learning styles, motivations, and needs; there is rigorous use of pupil target setting linked to high quality assessment; lessons are well paced and enjoyable; and pupils are supported by partnership with others well beyond the classroom.

'This is what I mean by "Personalised Learning". High expectation of every child, given practical form by high quality teaching based on a sound knowledge and understanding of each child's needs. It is not individualised learning where pupils sit alone at a computer. Nor is it pupils left to their own devices – which too often reinforces low aspirations. It can only be developed school by school. It cannot be imposed from above.'

Tips, ideas and activities

● Although it is unlikely that you will be the author of your school's Single Conversation, your part will be significant through your unique understanding of every child. Your input on intervention programmes and attainment strategies will provide much of the rationale that supports assessment results, which will be used to back up your school's Single Plan.

● There are five aspects to each single school plan: school improvement, teaching and learning, leadership and management, parents and community, and environment and premises. All aspects require complementary yet specific strategies if they are to coincide with the ultimate aim of improving children's attainment. Most of these aspects can be distilled to classroom level. A good classroom must be organised and have clearly signposted areas. Children should know where resources are kept and understand their part in organising and ordering their classroom environment. Children should expect clear lessons and it is reasonable for them to understand that you expect them to be ready to learn. Like yourself, it is not unreasonable for children to expect some sort of training to support their learning (particularly if this is a culture within your school). It may be how to lead reciprocal reading groups or how to peer mark each other's books but it should be an acknowledgment of their ability to learn different skills.

● Ultimately, any long-term review takes time to embed. It will take a certain amount of confidence to accept that any significant strategy will take up to two years before any trends and recurring impacts can be measured accurately. Your teaching and assessments will form just part of a child's learning journey.

You Can... **Understand Assessing Pupils' Progress**

Assessing Pupils' Progress (APP) is a broad assessment programme that allows the teacher to take assessment opportunities from any subject. APP is made up of a number of Assessment Focuses (AFs) that teachers use as a guide when matching evidence (which can be oral, written, formal or observational) in order to make a level judgement. This supports tracking across the year groups and allows teachers to identify strengths and areas for development.

Thinking points

● APP was first used in secondary schools. It has a proven track record of being robust, manageable and effective in practice.

● An advantage of APP is that it provides a forum for assessment opportunities that had previously remained anecdotal. Observations and conversations now form part of the evidence used for APP.

● APP is based on four key principles: assessment is integral to effective teaching and learning; assessment systems must be fit for purpose; national standards are an entitlement for learners, teachers and schools; national standards are integral to national expectations of education. These principles are not exclusive to APP, but APP takes the opportunity to draw them together. This is partly in response to an Ofsted observation that assessments did not sufficiently inform learning.

Tips, ideas and activities

● APP is most effective when you have good subject knowledge. If there is an aspect of the core curriculum that you know requires professional development, then speak to the appropriate curriculum leader. They should be able to arrange training either internally or externally.

● To use APP effectively, you will need appropriate training. To support any training, the National Strategy provides all the necessary materials on their website (nationalstrategies. standards.dcsf.gov.uk/primary/primaryframework/assessment/ app/). The site is regularly updated and will eventually include all of the Assessment Focuses (AFs), strategy guidelines, standards files and level judgement descriptors for maths, reading, writing, science, ICT and speaking and listening.

● Evidence can be gathered from across the whole curriculum. For example, a hot-seating activity in a history lesson may contribute to the body of evidence gathered for a literacy AF.

● APP is an intensive process, which is why it should only be carried out on a small group of children. However your ability to make accurate level judgements will grow.

● APP is designed to directly inform future planning, teaching and learning in the course of a year. It also helps you to fine-tune pupils' needs so that you can tailor the planning accordingly. The National Curriculum website defines the main purpose of APP as being to:
  ○ Track pupils' progress.
  ○ Use diagnostic information about pupils' strengths and weaknesses to improve teaching, learning and pupils' progress.
  ○ Make reliable judgements related to national standards drawing on a wide range of evidence.

You Can... Plan to implement Assessing Pupils' Progress

Assessing Pupils' Progress (APP) is a long-term assessment tool, rather than being the snapshot that a summative assessment provides. It works by reviewing a body of work created during a whole unit. To get the most from APP you may need to review how you plan in order to be able to create enough evidence to uphold any judgements. Given that the National Strategies have had a renewed focus on how lessons are planned – in extended units rather than five days – this is a timely opportunity to assess how you plan in order to make the most from both APP and the National Strategies.

Thinking points

● Before you use APP you will have had the appropriate training. It is not the type of tool that you can start using without proper guidance. However, once you start using the Assessment Focuses (AFs) with your focus group of children, the clarity of the process becomes evident. This skill can then be transferred to the other AFs.

● APP is a process of periodic review of work already done, not a new assessment event. As a basic principle, the reviewed work should cover more than one unit and at least one term's progress. This suggests that you will most likely formalise your judgements each term. You should not necessarily be planning to cover specific AFs in lessons, although this is not always inappropriate as some AFs have a specific focus, particularly in maths.

Tips, ideas and activities

● How and when you plan to implement APP will depend on your experience of the programme. If you are new or not secure in how it works then start with one strand. As with any programme, once you are familiar with how it operates you can begin to add new strands.

● Your focus group should reflect the range of abilities across your classroom. The core aim of APP is to fine-tune your ability in making concrete judgements and to that end your modal group should not reflect extremes within the classroom. Very able children can skew results and children who are very low attainers may have additional needs that are not necessarily educationally based.

● The time of year is important. Ideally, tracked children from the previous year will roll over and continue with your class in September so that the 'summer dip' can be tracked. Where the school has not agreed this, preferring to change the focus group each year, it is worth using the existing group for moderation purposes while you familiarise yourself with the new children.

● There is a natural cycle to the school year, starting in September. That said, there is a strong argument that suggests tracking children from April to April, as this embraces the summer dip and provides the opportunity to measure academic movement during your current year. Having assessed a child's standards, you will still have the summer to implement appropriate strategies if there are concerns. Also, this falls within the financial year and resources can be allocated more effectively during this calendar period.

You Can... **Plan to assess day to day**

Day-to-day assessments are based on daily interactions between pupil and teacher. These include discussions about their work, shared marking opportunities, conversations about their relationships with other children and how they reflect on their own assessment targets. It's within these conversations that a child reveals their depth of learning, whether they have grasped a concept or not, and if they have made links with other objectives or have learning misconceptions.

Thinking points

Children, particularly younger ones, can transfer skills and demonstrate that they have progressed in their understanding when it is presented in a different learning context. For example, pupils who lack confidence in number may create a better piece of work in an ICT lesson when the numbers are disguised as a chart or spreadsheet. Equally, children might produce better pieces of writing in history (particularly if it is a subject of specific interest) than in literacy. This may be down to confidence in the other subject or because a child is not expecting to be as closely assessed in these lessons. However, tracking assessment in other curriculum areas is a powerful way of showing a child their progress and building their confidence.

Tips, ideas and activities

● Day-to-day assessment should be embedded in planning, teaching and learning. This preparation will allow you and the child to get the most from the assessment opportunity.

● It requires a shared understanding of learning objectives and success criteria between teacher and pupil. When you first start using APP-style targets, you should clearly explain the targets to the child and revisit them as part of each assessment opportunity.

● Day-to-day assessments allow you the opportunity to identify evidence from a wide range of contexts.

● For many years, teachers have held a great deal of anecdotal evidence 'in their heads'. Including day-to-day assessment in your profiles gives value to this style of evidence and a forum in which to use it meaningfully.

● This style of assessment is based on evidence generated in the course of continuous teaching and learning, engagement with pupils through observation, discussion, questioning, and the review and analysis of work.

● This style of focused assessment will help to refine future plans, supporting the learning of the individual pupil. Spending time with a child helps them to recognise their successes and also helps them to celebrate and appreciate the hard work they are doing to meet their targets.

● Although children appreciate the attention that one-to-one interaction gives, it will actually promote independence and provide a stimulus for their self-motivation as they work towards achieving their targets.

● Practising this type of assessment will help a child to develop their ability for peer- and self-assessment as they emulate your strategies with other children, albeit at a child-appropriate level.

You Can... Plan to assess periodically

Assessing Pupils' Progress (APP) encourages periodic assessment of children's learning so you can make level judgements that are in line with national standards. Although day-to-day assessments can help to support your level judgements, it is important to take a step back from the whole process and review the learning that has taken place across the whole subject. Assessing periodically helps identify strengths and areas for development in groups and individuals, and can therefore inform future planning. It allows you to adapt planning for the individual child, thereby increasing the likelihood of them attaining their targets.

Thinking points

● Periodic assessment allows you to look at the big picture. A child may have uneven attainment across one subject area – this is not uncommon – and stepping back from the Assessment Focuses (AFs) allows you to take into consideration the whole child and their set of abilities. From this you may be able to refine your level judgement or at least rationalise why a child has made particular learning leaps or failed to move from a stubborn plateau.

● Periodic assessments use all assessment evidence available to the teacher, including summative as well as day-to-day assessment (although day-to-day evidence is likely to form the main body of evidence). The collection of evidence must have a purpose in order to meaningfully impact on future planning, which will depend on the aspect of the National Curriculum you are assessing. Ultimately, it must be fit for purpose to make best use of the time taken to assess.

Tips, ideas and activities

● Effective periodic assessment is based on current classroom activities – it should not be a complex additional assessment piece.

● The evidence required can come from a range of sources; it could be written, based on group observations (and how children interact), oral record or a piece of home learning.

● The assessment can be of a group or individual. In many cases, one piece of evidence – taken from how a group interacts – can meet the needs of several children. When you consider what evidence is available, written evidence reflects a limited percentage of a child's learning experience.

● Your assessment will have the most impact if the results can be used in future planning. As such, it requires planning and a clear link to current learning.

● Periodic assessment can reveal aspects of the curriculum that need strengthening. This can be either from the pupils' point of view or the teacher's. It may be that a particular aspect needs additional coverage.

● Periodic assessments can be used to direct discussions in parent consultations because they take into consideration a wider body of evidence than has traditionally been used. QCA-style year tests are still valid but are now only a proportional piece of evidence.

● Pupil conferences can have a broader focus when you are able to take into consideration all of the evidence available across all of the AFs. It is important that a child also has the opportunity to take time out and review their development.

● Analysing the outcomes of assessment can be an important tool in reviewing existing schemes of work by helping to identify where modification could lead to improvements.

You Can... Plan to assess at transition

Transition is a time when, historically, children dip in their performance. Three dips typically occur during primary education: Reception into Year 1, Year 2 into Year 3, and Year 6 into Year 7. Why this occurs is open to discussion but schools are increasingly aware of the need to accurately track children during these periods in order to ensure, as far as possible, a smooth learning journey. How you communicate with your colleagues and what information you share is important if your tracking is to be accurate and reflect the child's potential, not just National Curriculum Standards.

Thinking points

● Dips within education are natural. Children do not learn in convenient pathways. All kinds of events can create dips or peaks within learning, such as the birth of a sibling, parental separation, bereavement or moving house. Also, children can plateau.

● Although schools are conscious of the traditional transitional trends, an elongated plateau can take place between Years 3 and 5. During this time, some children, particularly boys, appear to make little progress before boosting during Year 5 and into Year 6. This is partly 'normal' and perhaps the result of a very long key stage. Key Stage 2 is the longest of all key stages from Foundation Stage to Key Stage 4.

● It is interesting to note that many schools are now beginning to create 'Phase' groups, effectively splitting Key Stage 2 into two equal phases, and QCA are also considering this change in the light of the renewed Primary Curriculum.

Tips, ideas and activities

● Planning is key to successful transition. Given the changes within the curriculum, announced in 2009 through the Primary Curriculum Review and Primary Review documents, your school will have an opportunity to review its curriculum. Review (if you have not already) how you plan to bridge the transition gaps between key phases and where there are known learning plateaus (such as between Years 4 and 5).

● If you can, plan with a colleague. It is at these times that you can, between you, refine the coming lessons and challenge the direction a lesson is taking.

● Talk to colleagues who have had the class in the past. They will be able to help you to interpret the tracking and explain any anomalies, such as a child dipping against prior attainment.

● How you track in school should immediately highlight any attainment changes. Most schools now use an electronic tracking system. There are several on the market (see page 56 for examples of market leaders). These programmes should identify transitional changes within the first term, giving you time to engage with the data rather than producing it.

● Using the Assessing Pupils' Progress (APP) materials will support successful judgements. It is best to use these materials when your subject knowledge is good. If there are gaps within your own subject knowledge, seek advice from a curriculum leader on any potential professional development opportunities either internally or externally.

● The APP assessment focus styles differ between subjects. Reading and writing tend to be more prescriptive than maths, which adopts a 'best fit' approach. These different styles impact on transitions between key year groups, so understanding how APP works is as important as subject knowledge if you are to avoid confusion between the level judgements.

You Can... Use Assessment Focuses

Assessment Focuses (AFs) are based on the National Curriculum level descriptions and programmes of study. They cover the areas for assessment, which lead on to the formal end-of-key-stage curriculum tests. Currently there are AFs for reading, writing and maths but by 2010 there will be similar tools for speaking and listening, ICT and science. The AFs provide an ongoing opportunity for assessment within a primary classroom, unlike end-of-year or key stage tests, which give a snapshot sample of attainment achieved within the primary curriculum. Both types of assessment form evidence to support your level judgement.

Thinking points

● AFs sit between the National Curriculum Programmes of Study (PoS) and their level descriptions. As such, they provide much more detail on what is expected from a child at any given level. This detail, however, is not meant as additional learning objectives because the evidence to support your judgements should come from the National Curriculum. As the AFs emerge between the National Curriculum PoSs and the Strategy documents for maths and literacy, you will notice that there are specific skills that appear within the AFs that will need some specific planning, should you wish to include them as part of your level judgement. Using AFs in this way should be the exception as this is not their function. Knowing what AFs you are aiming to meet within a unit of work can subtly direct questioning and learning opportunities.

Tips, ideas and activities

● The original pilot programme defined the benefits of AFs as:
  ● Providing diagnostic information on pupils' strengths and weaknesses in relation to specific assessment focuses.
  ● Enabling forward planning based on group and individual pupil needs.
  ● Making the most of pupils' learning experiences across the whole curriculum. (*APP Handbook 2007* © QCA, 2007, for use by pilot schools only (v4 01-07-07)).

● Using AFs will help you develop a good understanding of the common requirements of all National Curriculum levels.

● Each AF has two or three bullet points at every level. These criteria identify what you, when observing, should be looking for in a pupil's work. By measuring a small number of criteria you will begin to see what the big picture is for that child (or group) in terms of progress and possible attainment.

● The AFs will support you in giving precise feedback to pupils, which is particularly important when devising learning journeys (see pages 22 and 60). Ofsted are now interested in whether a child knows what they need to do in order to achieve a target.

● The AFs will help you to identify learning gaps and improve the focus of group/individual learning targets.
● The chart below shows how AFs fit into the daily routine:

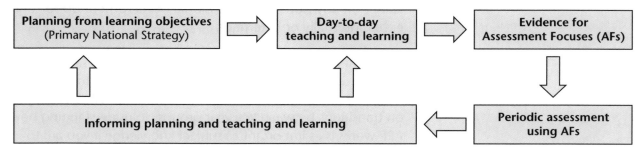

Planning from learning objectives (Primary National Strategy)	→	Day-to-day teaching and learning	→	Evidence for Assessment Focuses (AFs)
↑		↑		↓
Informing planning and teaching and learning			←	Periodic assessment using AFs

You Can... Use Assessment Focuses in literacy

Literacy is the backbone to all learning and as such has been broken down into three manageable learning strands: reading, writing, and speaking and listening. Because of this the Assessment Focuses (AFs) guidance for reading and writing makes a number of points that should be considered before you start using AFs for literacy (speaking and listening will be available by 2010 and is likely to have similar suggestions).

Thinking points

● Literacy is dependent on a grasp of the English language. Where English is not a child's first language other assessment models should be taken into consideration before you begin to use AFs. Typically, scales of language acquisition, such as the four-stage Hester Scale based on the work by Hilary Hester, are necessary filters before applying AFs or making a judgement. In these cases a bigger picture has to be taken into consideration. A child may have good literacy skills within their own language, which are masked by their level of English acquisition.

● Literacy's impact goes well beyond the National Strategy lessons. Every class assembly, lesson in history, geography, RE, science, ICT, and so on provides opportunities for meaningful literacy assessment opportunities. It is not unreasonable to use these opportunities, in a cross-curricular way, to plan to cover an AF that can be later used when gathering evidence to make your Assessing Pupils' Progress (APP) level judgement.

Tips, ideas and activities

● Reading AFs:
  ● AFs are not hierarchical, age or ability related, and they define broad areas in which evidence can be examined in order to determine how well pupils are progressing.
  ● Readers use a range of strategies to decode texts (AF1) which become more automatic with experience, as listening to pupils read throughout Key Stage 2 demonstrates.
  ● Reading involves making meaning from content, structure and language (AFs 2–5).
  ● To develop as readers who can make sense of a wide range of texts, pupils need to be secure on AF3. Securing AF3 underpins progress through level 4 and above.
  ● The AFs which highlight evaluation and analysis (AFs 4–7) build on the skills in AFs 1–3.
  ● In exploring a text, readers respond to specific aspects (AFs 4–5) and to the text as a whole (AF6) and consider how the text relates to their wider experience (AF7).

● Writing AFs:
  ● Writing is a complex, unitary skill, so these elements are interactive and interdependent even though they can each be analysed.
  ● The different facets of writing develop together: when teaching specific aspects of grammar it is important to show how they relate to writing as a whole.
  ● Pupils need to learn how to orchestrate skills at word, sentence and text level in order to be able to write independently.
  ● When assessing it is important to look at the parts in relation to text as a whole, for example how individual sentences contribute to overall effect.
  ● Some evidence may relate to more than one assessment focus, for example AF1 and AF3.
  ● There is **not** an AF for handwriting and presentation, but guidance about how to assess these features is available for National Curriculum levels 1–3.

You Can... Use Assessment Focuses in maths

Unlike reading or writing, maths tends to be a discrete subject. This is reflected in the Primary Review *and* Primary Curriculum Review *(both cite maths as the only subject that should be taught discretely). As such the maths Assessment Focuses (AFs) are set out slightly differently from those for literacy. The four maths attainment targets are now subdivided into approximately 14 AFs. This might sound excessive but reading and writing have fifteen between them, with more to be added when speaking and listening comes online during 2010.*

Thinking points

● The AFs for maths go into much more detail than the National Curriculum or Strategy documents. The temptation, therefore, is to use the AFs as a lesson objective. While this ensures coverage of the AF and provides evidence to substantiate a judgement, it is not the intention of the programme. Planning led by an AF objective should be the exception rather than the norm.

● Number (Attainment target Ma2) is the dominant AF and as such requires the widest range of evidence. It is recommended that you start with this, as it will require the most time to source evidence.

Tips, ideas and activities

● Spend time getting to know the AFs. This will enable you to match planning with AF assessment opportunities rather than trying to fill gaps later in the year. It will also mean that the evidence created by the children is relevant and reflects the standards described in the AFs. The AFs match the National Curriculum and are not intended to substitute it.

● Be clear about what counts as evidence. Observation (either group or individual), formal test, photocopied work, and peer marking can all count as evidence.

● Although not recommended, you should be prepared to adapt or adjust your planning in order to meet the requirements of an AF.

● Be prepared to allow children to lead their own learning. Ongoing assessments will offer regular opportunities in which children lead their own learning, which are useful for observation. Observing a group undertaking an activity is as useful as leading an activity yourself, as it can highlight learning gaps as well as providing evidence to support an assessment judgement.

● Step back and allow children to choose the resources they feel they need. This is part of the assessment process, and what they choose can be revealing. It also allows you to celebrate individuals who make appropriate use of the resources. If your school is new to Assessing Pupils' Progress (APP), it is useful if everyone starts with the same AF. This allows colleagues the time to get to know one area of maths and provides time to discuss issues arising from it (formally in meetings or informally), before taking on the whole programme.

You Can... **Use the assessment guidelines**

The assessment guidelines are the criteria for each level and the key document of Assessing Pupils' Progress (APP). These sheets help you to assess pupils' work in relation to national standards, and provide a simple recording format for the assessment criteria in each of the Assessment Focuses (AFs) for the subject at each level. This is where you use the evidence collected, be it oral, observational or written, to form a level judgement. Currently, guidelines exist for levels 2–5 in reading, writing and maths, with overview descriptions of levels 2–8 in both maths and English. Additional guidelines are planned for the near future.

Thinking points

● Assessment guidelines are extremely personal. Each level assessment is designed to be used for one child and draws together all of the relevant AFs for each subject (including handwriting and presentation in the writing guidelines).

● There is no common format for the guidelines. Maths is set out in a very different style to the reading and writing guidelines. Maths looks for a best-fit level description, whereas reading and writing are looking for an accurate record. All three, however, use the same language of 'low', 'secure' and 'high' when describing a child's level description.

● The AFs listed for reading and writing are not in order. This does not reflect any final level description but you should be aware of this anomaly when talking with colleagues.

Tips, ideas and activities

● The guidelines enable teachers to see a pupil's 'profile' of attainment and to share this with colleagues, the child and parents. When sharing the guidelines with different audiences, avoid jargon. It is a fine line between confusing listeners with professional terminology and sounding authoritative.

● The guidelines provide a basis for discussing targets for improvement with pupils, parents and carers, based on the results you have input.

● Previously, it has been difficult to quantify sub-level progress within a level descriptor, as descriptors cover the whole level and not part of it. The assessment guidelines are designed to allow progress to be seen within the level and provide accurate sub-level descriptors that can be matched against ability and the evidence you use. A useful way of annotating work that you are using as evidence is to copy the individual objectives onto mini sticky-notes (as used on envelopes and available in A4 sheets). Once created, you can add them to your evidence along with the date and any additional commentary. The evidence can be stored on a computer and used across the school – a good administration officer will be able to cut and paste from the original document!

● Highlighting assessments has become common practice in many schools and is an effective and quick way of assessing a child's ability because assessments show at a glance, and also the standards not achieved stand out clearly. This helps the process of assessing whether there is enough evidence to conclude a judgement.

● The assessment guidelines can be found at the National Standards website, www.nationalstrategies.standards.dcsf.gov.uk/primary (once on this page, click on 'APP' under the Assessment title). Each set is available as a PDF and should open on most computers, mobile phones and hand-held devices.

You Can... Gather evidence and observe

There are essentially three types of evidence you can collect to form the whole package of evidence needed to ratify an Assessment Focus (AF): spoken (oral), written and observed. Together, these give a complete picture of a child's attainment. This is a clear move away from a reliance on just test-based results and an ideal vehicle for using all the evidence that teachers have – for generations – kept in their heads. How it is captured is the key to turning what you have heard or observed into a useful piece of evidence.

Thinking points

● Interestingly, test-based assessments have recently had a resurgence through computer programs. As most tests can be created to have finite answers, a computer is able to quickly calculate the total score and present a test scrutiny almost instantly. But this does not reveal how well a child works within a group or how well they are able to communicate to their peers. Nor does it assess deeper understanding. Computer-based tests are, in almost the crudest terms, snapshots that present useful but limited data.

● Gathering evidence should be a shared activity, not just down to you. It is useful to delegate part of the responsibility to another adult in your classroom. Observations can be labour-intensive or even impossible if you are working alongside the group during the activity. Teachers and Early Years practitioners (nursery nurses) have worked like this for many years and are worth approaching for professional support.

Tips, ideas and activities

● Collecting oral evidence requires planning. There are good quality, economic voice recorders on the market, for example TTS generally has a good range on their website. These can be used to record what a child is saying, such as during a science investigation explanation. Increasing numbers of these recorders contain integrated USB ports that allow you to download straight to the computer and review immediately. This has the added advantage of allowing a child to interact with the assessment as soon as it has been created as well as being a useful piece of evidence.

● Photocopies of pieces of work are classic evidence. They should include a commentary explaining the context of the work and, ideally, any additional points.

● Agree a common collection format – most likely a set of folders for each child. Without having an agreed place to file your evidence it could be lost or damaged.

● Photographs are a very useful way of catching the moment. Most class teachers have access to a digital camera and may have one as part of their phone. Most schools have a photography policy or seek parental permission, so check to see if there is anyone you cannot photograph in your class. These are not professional photographs but they have a specific use in your evidence file as long as they present clear evidence of success.

● Annotated planning can also form part of your evidence-base and it may be your only record of evidence.

● It is useful to have a set of sticky labels to write on when you are observing a child. This is common practice in Foundation Stage and is a transferable skill for APP assessments. Keeping sticky labels to hand allows you to collect both planned and informal evidence as it happens.

You Can... **Make a level judgement in maths**

Historically, maths is a 'black and white' assessment process – either they have it or they don't. But that does not take into consideration the processes a child goes through in order to find an answer or the conversations they might be part of. Assessing Pupils' Progress (APP) considers these processes to be valuable evidence. We now have to rethink how we make our level judgements and what evidence to include, for example a conversation that you overheard could be that valuable piece of evidence you were looking for.

Thinking points

● Consider what resources you have in school. Will they allow you to undertake all the necessary observations needed to compile a portfolio of maths evidence for your focus pupil? For example, do you have enough Cuisenaire rods in the box and do all the calculators work? Effective planning in partnership with APP will allow you to find out and have enough time to collect the necessary equipment.

● Making a level judgement is the focus of APP. That does not mean you can use it exclusively as your assessment procedure. Indeed, APP alone will not provide the range of evidence needed to secure a level judgement. As one consultant commented, you can have AfL without APP but not the other way round.

Tips, ideas and activities

● Look at the range of evidence for mathematics for the pupil you have chosen. Is it sufficient to begin the process of making a level judgement? For APP, sampling of work should pinpoint what is most significant for the pupil. It is not a portfolio of all the pupil has done but the evidence must be enough to secure a judgement. The National Strategies website provides examples of the types of evidence required to make a judgement.

● If not already completed, do the APP guideline for this child and, using the flowchart, determine the overall level. The flowchart will help you identify where there is insufficient evidence or where the child has underperformed.
Discuss your judgements with colleagues in your phase group or year group to check consistency of judgements.

● Moderate the level where necessary using the APP level descriptors.
Effective planning from the National Curriculum and the Primary Framework lays the foundation for the APP approach to assessment. You may need to modify some planning in order to cover enough targets to make a judgement.

● Effective evidence draws on different contexts. This helps to show how the standard of pupils' work is maintained or how it varies in different situations with different degrees of support, for example how the focus pupil applies maths in science or in ICT lessons. Does their knowledge of number transcend other subjects?

● Effective evidence comes from different types of assessment, including spoken, written, extended work, notes and jottings, as well as from teacher observations and conversations with the pupil. This is a new aspect for maths as it was historically based on written evidence. Now, how children talk and think about maths are just as important, and are arguably more useful life skills.

You Can... Make a level judgement in reading

Reading is used in every aspect of the curriculum; it could be a poem in literacy, an account of the Great Fire of London or a maths problem. How children read and for what purpose are at the core of the curriculum. As such, you will have an abundant source of evidence available. Many of the Assessment Focuses (AFs) can be covered with careful planning rather than by relying purely on literacy lessons for evidence, although the core of your assessment is still likely to come from literacy.

Thinking points
● The goal of reading is to help children to learn to love books – at all levels and in all contexts – and therefore to create a lifelong learning skill. Assessment should seek to understand what strategies the child has, what they need to improve and how that can be done. Assessing Pupils' Progress (APP) is just one tool that will support you and your children in this process. Always consider if the texts are appropriate, for example: do they stretch the child you are assessing and are there a reasonable range of texts so that they can transfer their reading skills as they improve?

● Assessment systems must be 'fit for purpose' and provide meaningful data. There must also be a balance between time taken evaluating assessments and time spent on developing good quality lessons. Reading is a good example of where clear planning across the curriculum can provide meaningful evidence efficiently.

Tips, ideas and activities
● Before starting to make a level judgement, the Standards site suggests you will need:
  ○ Evidence of the pupil's reading that shows most independence.
  ○ Other evidence about the pupil as a reader, for example notes on plans, the pupil's own reflections, your own recollections of classroom interactions.
  ○ A copy of the assessment guidelines for the level borderline that is your starting point.

● Start your process by making a best-fit judgement. Use your personal experience and evidence of the child's reading skill to decide whether they are for the higher or lower AF. This does not necessarily mean they fulfil the AF; it's simply just a best-fit starting place before you begin the finer analysis.

● Highlight the criteria the child has met. This will make the form easier to read when finalising your judgement. At this point, if you do not have enough reading evidence then it is important to state the fact.

● There are seven AFs for reading (deduction, explanation, strategies, understanding, structure, use of language and how texts relate culturally) and each will require an assessment. Each requires evidence and where there is insufficient evidence it will need to be identified on the sheet as this will have implications for future planning. The guidelines for marking as assessment can be found at www.nationalstrategies.standards. dcsf.gov.uk/node/20683.

● To make a level judgement you will need to review all seven AFs and evaluate their spread. The National Literacy Strategy gives examples of what needs to be covered so that a secure judgement can be made (see: http://nationalstrategies. standards.dcsf.gov.uk/primary/primaryframework/assessment/ app/mj/reading).

You Can... Make level a judgement in writing

Out of all the core subjects, writing is the area that requires the most long-term planning. Most Year 6 teachers will be able to tell you that maths, science and reading can be boosted to higher levels (arguably superficially) in the short term for end-of-key-stage assessments but that it is far harder to do the same in writing. Why this is the case has been debated and analysed for years but, in simple terms, writing is difficult. It is a sophisticated skill that requires practice. Level judgements in this subject also require as much practice on your part, a long with solid evidence to support them.

Thinking points

● How we write is changing dramatically. The National Strategy for Literacy has done much to even out the balance of fiction and non-fiction writing, giving children a purpose behind their writing. But many schools are now taking writing into a new arena where children use laptops (or web-books as the new generation of small, cheap laptops are called) to compose and write. This is no bad thing as it is preparing a child for modern working conditions when they leave school. However, the speed at which they type is unlikely to match the speed at which they can write with a pen. The trade-off is that children do not need to worry about presentation, and spelling/grammatical errors are clearer on a screen, but there is still some way to go before keyboards replace pens at primary levels, simply because pens are more convenient.

Tips, ideas and activities

● Before starting to make a writing level judgement the Standards site suggests you will need:
  ● Evidence of the pupil's writing that shows most independence, for example from a range of subjects outside of direct literacy teaching.
  ● Other evidence about the pupil as a writer, for example notes on plans, the pupil's own reflections, your own recollections of classroom interactions.
  ● A copy of the assessment guidelines for the level borderline that is your starting point.

● Writing has eight Assessment Focuses (AFs). Do you have enough evidence to cover these AFs in order to make your judgement? There are no AFs for presentation, although the Standards site does provide advice. There is, however, one AF for handwriting which is still part of the end-of-key-stage assessment tests.

● Start your process by making a best-fit judgement. Use your personal experience and evidence of the child's writing skill to decide whether they are for the higher or lower AF. This does not necessarily mean they fulfil the AF; it's simply a best-fit starting place before you begin the finer analysis.

● Highlight the criteria the child has met. This will make the form easier to read when finalising your judgement. At this point, if you do not have enough writing evidence then it is important to state the fact.

● To make a level judgement you will need to review all eight AFs and evaluate their spread. The Strategy gives examples of what needs to be covered so that a secure judgement can be made (found at nationalstrategies.standards.dcsf.gov.uk/node/18050).

You Can... Get the most from using the standards files

Once your school is familiar with using Assessing Pupils' Progress (APP), you will have created a selection of levelled children's work that you can use when moderating assessments from children. By comparing work against formally moderated work, you can begin to answer questions such as: Has this child achieved a low level 3? What would a similar, moderated piece look like, and what would be the criteria for making this low rather than secure? To support this process, and until you have an agreed body of moderated work, the Standards site has a number of moderated pieces exemplifying levelled work.

Thinking points

● The APP standards files have a final link on the right-hand table titled 'Using the training standards files'. These documents have been created without annotation and are for training purposes. Having been moderated, they can be used with groups of staff to show the process of making a level judgement. Equally, during the process of making a secure level judgement you can look at these examples of moderated work against evidence pieces that a child may have created.

● The standards files are useful when you have no other moderated work that uses the APP framework to judge against. Once you are familiar with the whole APP process you will not necessarily need to use these exemplars as much as when you started. That said, they are a useful resource when an external piece of moderated work is needed.

Tips, ideas and activities

● The standards files can be accessed from: www.standards.dcsf.gov.uk/primaryframework/assessment/standards_files or by searching for 'Standards Files' at www.nationalstrategies.standards.dcsf.gov.uk.

● This section of the website is divided into seven topic areas located in the tab section on the right-hand side of the page. To access pupil exemplars, first select the subject you are moderating. A further drop-down table will appear giving the name of each child and the level aspect their piece of work exemplifies. Select the appropriate child's name to continue. Alternatively, you can select the subject, which will present a table that shows the pupil, their attainment level and how this compares with all the attainment strands. For example, Saleema, a maths level 3 child, is judged to be overall secure despite one of the strands giving a judgement of low.

● All of the standards files exemplars are in PDF format. Your computer, most likely, will allow you to open these documents when you download them (a PDF is a common format and downloads like a Word document).

● Each of the exemplars, when opened, will give the subject, level aspect (low, secure, high), a thumbnail image of the child's work, teacher's note, next steps, what the teacher knows about the child and a summary of the child's attainment. For additional information a teacher can access the full commentary. This can be downloaded as a PDF file at the top of the page. These notes are exemplars and, as such, are more thorough than would be expected in the classroom.

You Can... **Understand what the Improving Schools Programme is**

The Improving Schools Programme (ISP) is designed to raise standards and improve teaching and learning in the context of the school as a professional learning community. It is based on the cycle of audit and setting targets, action and review, with four key themes running through the programme: raising standards and accelerating progress; improving the quality of teaching and learning; improving the conditions for learning; and developing the school as a learning community. A fifth theme, leadership, acts as an overarching element, ensuring continuity and building in the capacity to develop future leaders.

Thinking points

● The ISP was originally developed for schools with low attainment or where groups of children who were not achieving as expected were identified. However, the programme can be tailored to meet the needs of most schools as it relies on the school's existing systems and embodies the core principles of assessment. The benefit of the ISP is that it is both highly structured (see non-negotiables on page 40 and Raising Attainment Plans page 41) and flexible enough to respond to change.

● The ISP relies on senior leadership being accountable for its success. It is their role to disseminate responsibility to middle leaders. By having this top-down approach (starting with the local authority), leadership capacity can be enhanced at all levels, allowing the programme to act as a meaningful tool for professional development.

Tips, ideas and activities

● The ISP involves the whole school community but especially the headteacher and senior leadership team, school governors, middle leaders, teachers, parents and children. The local authority is also involved in partnership with the School Improvement Partner.

● Running alongside the current curriculum changes, the ISP supports curriculum review and the provision of a curriculum that meets the needs and interests of all learners. This is in line with *Every Child Matters* and reflects current thinking.

● Teachers and schools are confronted with a wide range of different assessment programmes (this book examines three of the most significant but there are many more circulating). The ISP sets out to establish a clear set of protocols that teachers can use as part of their reflections during the progression of the programme. You should find time to evaluate your current procedures and analyse the ISP's impact on your practice and pupils. This is a key aspect of the professional development that is woven into the programme.

● As with any programme, you will need professional development. Good assessment analysis is reliant on strong subject knowledge and an understanding of the programme you are using.

● To find out more about the ISP go to www.standards.dfes. gov.uk/primary/wholeschool/isp or, for case studies, go to www.whatworkswell.standards.dcsf.gov.uk.

You Can... Understand the non-negotiables

The Improving Schools Programme (ISP) cycle begins with a specific audit referred to as 'the audit of non-negotiables'. The non-negotiable audit establishes a common basis for the school. These non-negotiables give the headteacher and local authority consultant a clear view of the strengths and areas for development against the four key themes (see below). It is a baseline from which the rest of the programme cycle develops. Non-negotiables influence the development of the Raising Attainment Plan (see page 41), the range of professional development meetings and class-based action and, ultimately, the review.

Thinking points

● A core element of the Improving Schools Programme (ISP) is the identification of excellent practice and the development of colleagues through structured Professional Development Meetings. The ISP guidelines explain that the overarching aim is to create a 'programme based on the establishment of key systems in the participating schools, which will provide a coherent approach to raising standards and support the schools in becoming self-sustaining professional learning communities'. (*Introducing the ISP booklet*)

● Non-negotiables ensure appropriate target-setting and pupil-tracking systems are properly in place before the programme begins. This allows the school to clearly track attainment across the school, thereby providing an indicator of the programme's overall impact. It is important that you understand how to unpick your pupil data from an electronic report. This may be the first area for development within your school because it is essential that you and your colleagues are able to use the data at your disposal.

Tips, ideas and activities

● A non-negotiable audit consists of four key themes (which run throughout ISP):
1. Raising standards and accelerating progress.
2. Quality of teaching and learning.
3. Improving the conditions for learning.
4. Developing the school as a professional learning community.

● These themes form the headings for each section of the audit, which are then punctuated with questions designed to lead the audit trail. Evidencing these forms the rationale for the rest of the programme's cycle as it should highlight the school's various strengths and areas for development.

● Key theme 2, the quality of teaching and learning, often elicits the most apprehension from teachers as it makes direct references to their planning and lesson observation. However, when sensitively done and in direct response to appropriate professional development, it is a powerful element of the ISP, and should be structured with clear goals and timeframes.

● An audit of non-negotiables can be downloaded from: www.lgfl.net/lgfl/leas/camden/accounts/primary/ISP/NonNegiotables.

● Each audit for each school is different because of the complex variety of skills, personnel and resources available to any establishment. The audit is a good opportunity to engage with key theme 3 and open the discussion to other core stakeholders, including pupils and parents. Increasingly, learning is moving beyond the classroom and schools are taking creative advantage of their outside learning spaces for older years. This is common practice in Wales, which has a dedicated woodlands programme for many of its schools.

You Can... Write a Raising Attainment Plan

A Raising Attainment Plan (RAP) is a working document that ties the whole ISP process together. It should be written after a school audit and its core purpose is to monitor the progress made by the school and to evaluate the procedures being used. Unlike most action plans, it should be reviewed termly by the school leadership team and ISP consultant (usually a local authority representative). This document underpins the long-term action of the school and should, therefore, be written with due care.

Thinking points

An RAP has a purposefully short life. Its aim is to tie the four key themes of the ISP programme (see below) into a document that constantly demands attention from all levels of leadership because of the restricted time limits. A term may sound like a reasonable length of time but in busy schools, where time is precious, the weeks can fly by. However, once familiar with the ISP cycle, and when attainment levels are seen to visibly improve (as they have done in many schools) the tight time frames emerge as a necessary challenge. The timing of the RAP is easier to manage where schools have balanced terms (this is the case for most London schools where the Easter weekend is not absorbed into the second term if it falls early rather than marking the end of a very short term).

● Four key themes should be addressed within the RAP as part of the focused intervention strategy:

   ● Raising standards and accelerating progress.

   ● Improving the quality of teaching and learning.

   ● Improving the conditions for learning.

   ● Developing the school as a professional learning community. (Intensifying Support Programme DfES 0037-2004).

Tips, ideas and activities

● When writing an RAP, aim to keep your language clear and succinct to avoid ambiguous statements.

● Success criteria should be linked to clear targets, and set out what the school is aiming to achieve.

● Make time scales clear. This will help the school to keep the targets in focus. Ensure that individuals are aware of their specific roles and what aspects of the RAP they are responsible for when monitoring.

● Targets should be specific such as '10 per cent uplift in African boys' attainment'. Targets should relate to learning, progress and summative attainment.

● A local authority consultant will help you write your RAP, which will be based on the identified non-negotiables.

● A clear difference between a standard action plan and an RAP is the inclusion of an objective. Although schools are increasingly referring to a school vision by writing action plans, an objective clarifies what the school is aiming to achieve and the necessary success criteria.

● Action plans must be manageable if they are to be successful. This boosts morale and supports the school's involvement with the ISP.

● The school and the local authority consultant should review the RAP at the end of each year. This should be a rigorous process, as any successive RAP will be influenced by the success of its predecessor.

You Can... Create Improving Schools Programme tables and tools

Tracking individuals is key to the success of the Improving Schools Programme (ISP) and positively reflects the Every Child Matters agenda. As a result, the programme has created a range of tools to support tracking procedures. They are designed to engage the professional with a child's data, supporting a dialogue about pupil progress, groupings, expectations and appropriate use of interventions. They form the backbone to the range of data available to teachers (such as RAISEOnline, the Fischer Family Trust and other electronic assessment tools) that create a whole picture of the individual child's attainment.

Thinking points

● With experience it is possible to quickly identify trends or patterns occurring across the year, particularly plateaus or where children are not learning at an expected rate. There may be external factors (such as parental separation or moving home) but, when recognised, trends should provide evidence for intervention programmes in order to raise standards.

● See page 58 for a photocopiable page that can be used to support the tracking of attainment across a year. On its own it is a useful device for a group of specific children but it should be converted into a Microsoft Word® or Excel® document if you wish to use it for a class or cohort. To translate it into a working document, entry levels should be grey and end-of-year levels yellow.

Tips, ideas and activities

● Colour coding the tracking system allows you to quickly scan children who are attaining age-related expectations. Equally, it is useful to colour-code children who achieved level 3 (eg red font) at the end of KS1 and those who achieved below level 2b (eg blue font). When a child's name is plotted the colour-coded name will quickly show if a child's attainment is as predicted. Typically, a range of two sub-levels for each year group would accurately reflect attainment.

● Many electronic tracking systems, such as TargSats or Target Tracker, have ISP colours embedded into them. However, it is possible to create a simplified tool (either as a Word or Excel document) by following these guidelines:

  ○ Ensure you know the national expectations for the end of each academic year. Typically, this will be an increment of two-thirds of a level from the previous year. This can be refined to a termly prediction where a child would be expected to remain at the end of the previous year's level in term one and to improve by one-third of a level during each of the next two terms. This is not always the case but is a good guideline.

  ○ Identify appropriate groups of children who would benefit from directed support. This should be based on current understanding, your prior knowledge of their ability and predicted attainment. This will provide evidence of progress across the cohort.

  ○ Set challenging, but realistic, targets for the end of the year. Target groups, in particular, should be set especially challenging targets in order to support the investment of additional intervention and draw them back into line with expectation and age-related results.

You Can... **Work in partnership with your local authority**

The Improving Schools Programme (ISP) sets out to integrate all interested parties, from the children to the local authority, into one body. There are six areas of intervention that the local authority and school work together on. Your input as a class teacher will adapt with the level of professional development and local authority partnership work. It is a partnership that has the core belief that all children are entitled to reach national expectations.

Thinking points

The traditional position of the local authority as moderator and light-touch inspector does not necessarily apply to the ISP model. It is a partnership that has the central aim of improving individual standards (as measured by the ISP tables and supported by intervention strategies where standards are below expectations) through a shared plan and dialogue. That said, the conversation benefits from an external perspective that can, without prejudice, add a professional level of challenge. This is not always comfortable but the model has proved to be extremely successful with many schools. Challenge is a necessary aspect of the profession and should be viewed as an opportunity to sharpen your practice as this should lead to improved standards. Naturally, it is often easier to appreciate the benefits after the event!

Tips, ideas and activities

● Effective pupil tracking systems are designed to stimulate a professional dialogue between you and your local authority representative. The ISP tables should identify trends and needs. Importantly, though, they are not designed to act as a crude way of creating groups. This could lead to the lowering of standards, and it will be within the remit of your line manager or local authority representative to challenge this.

● Strategic whole-school curricular target setting supports the school in understanding and knowing about standards, beyond NC levels. It is a shared focus that allows each child to learn where they are on their learning journey and what they need to do in order to progress. Your local authority representative will also be looking at tactical use of curricular target setting for specific, hard-to-learn core curriculum objectives. At this point, Wave 2 or 3 interventions may be suggested.

● Your local authority representative will be able to access specific Wave 2 and Wave 3 intervention materials. Wave 2 interventions, such as Y6 Booster groups, are specifically aimed at children attaining just below national expectations. Wave 3 interventions focus on small groups or individuals who are performing at well-below age-related expectations.

● Professional Development Meetings (PDMs) form the ongoing heart of the ISP year. This is where you will have greatest access to your local authority representative, who will generally run most of the sessions. It is a good opportunity to get to know them and develop your working relationship, and will aid your conversations when analysing pupil progress.

● Pupil progress meetings are an opportunity to review the impact of any intervention programmes on a child and to develop your teacher assessment skills. They generally last for an hour and should involve a high degree of challenge, professional dialogue and target setting. The results set new outcomes that might form part of the next RAP.

You Can... **Write a living policy**

Assessment, at heart, is a dialogue between several groups of people: children, parents/carers, governors, colleagues, local authority and national bodies. It is easy to draft a policy that details all the individual assessment programmes used by the school (such as APP, AfL, ISP, formal testing, standardised testing, day-to-day) and miss the whole point of assessment. Essentially, assessment should identify a child's prior learning, form meaningful and challenging targets, communicate and agree these targets with appropriate stakeholders, adapt planning, and evaluate the process in order to assess progression.

Thinking points

● Internationally, England is unique at offering optional formal assessments for year groups in Years 3 to 5. It is almost alone within Europe in publishing results and is the only country to currently publish results as league tables. Internationally, there is a growing movement towards league tables and standardised testing. However, England is only one of the three European countries that assess children at entry in Reception.

● The report *2020 Vision: Report of the Teaching and Learning in 2020 Review Group* identified five core strategies that have had an impact on standards: 1) Engineering effective discussions, questions and tasks that elicit evidence of learning; 2) Providing feedback that moves learners forward; 3) Clarifying and sharing learning intentions and criteria for success; 4) Activating children as the owners of their own learning; 5) Activating children as resources for one another. These are solid strategies that should be reflected within an assessment policy.

Tips, ideas and activities

● It is difficult to create a short assessment policy, and in many cases this is not necessarily appropriate given the importance of this aspect of school life. However, in order to create a document that your families can digest, it is good practice to develop a single page 'headline' document of the full policy. This document will be easier to circulate and amend as trends change within the school. It should include core assessment aims and how they are communicated to families.

● An assessment policy should be regularly reviewed. Given the recent and significant changes to assessment (since 2002 there have been three major assessment programmes compared to one partial review of the curriculum – the revised strategies), the standard three-year governors' policy review cycle may need to be shortened. In most cases you will only need to 'tweak' your policy, but the document should be dated and signed as an update by your Chair of Governors and it should reflect current assessment practice.

● Most schools include their assessment policy on their website. This is a good place to put the full document as it keeps it in the public forum. If you are writing a new policy, a web search for 'primary assessment policy' will provide examples of existing policies from other schools. They may not reflect your school's aims but they are a useful starting point.

● A policy should be clearly written, succinct and should reflect current practice. Suggested main headings could be:
  ● Assessment principles.
  ● Communication.
  ● Leadership (including governance).
  ● How it reflects the school's aims/vision.
  ● Assessment procedures.

You Can... **Explain your assessment to governors**

How we assess has changed dramatically over the last few years. Assessment for Learning, Assessing Pupils' Progress and electronic assessment tools such as RAISEOnline are just three examples of complex changes that many teachers are struggling to keep up with. For governors it can be a minefield and they will turn to schools to lead them intelligently so that they can continue to perform their role, as critical friend, with due diligence.

Thinking points

● Whether intentionally or not, it is all too easy to slip into using professional jargon. When it is necessary to use technical terms, it is important that you can make yourself understood by your audience. Your governors will want to know that you – in whatever role you hold within the school – are conversant with current thinking, but they will also need to understand what you are talking about. Acronyms should be explained the first time you use them and it is generally useful to start any report with a brief rationale. You want your governors to be able to govern effectively, not be overpowered by terminology.

● Your governing body are entitled to a number of training days each year as part of the school's agreement with the local authority. Given the focus on assessment, you may want to suggest this as the subject of a training session. The more informed your governors are the better they will be able to support the school.

Tips, ideas and activities

● Target setting is now commonplace in most schools (page 41 describes a range of target-setting models). As the teacher, your role is to support parents in unpicking what the assessment targets are and what needs to be done to achieve the goals. Ofsted now asks children: a) what is your target and, b) what do you need to do in order to achieve it? If you are clear in your mind about this information and have shared it with the parent/carers, the chances of each child's exposure to appropriate learning opportunities are increased.

● Be careful not to use too many acronyms or jargon when talking to parents. However well informed the parent or carer may be, the teaching profession is littered with terminology that most professionals can barely keep up with. If you do have to use acronyms, such as SEN, then explain what the acronym means and ensure you use it in an appropriate context.

● Using translators is now commonplace in most urban schools, reflecting the multicultural intake of children. There are extreme examples (some schools in London boast over a hundred different nationalities), but generally one or two languages will dominate. Arranging a translation service not only demonstrates a school's commitment to that family but also ensures that assessments are understood when shared. Knowing who speaks the community language within your school can prove to be invaluable if you need to talk to a parent quickly.

● Be sensitive when timing your conversation. If you have a genuine concern then it is appropriate to agree a meeting with the parents rather than to bring it up in conversation in the playground. It is reasonable to briefly explain why you would like to see them and professional to assume that your conversation will not be held in public.

You Can... Track assessment across the school

An assessment leader will need to be able to track pupils across the school in order to identify trends. Trends are likely to vary between cohorts, but your systems should be robust enough to provide the big picture whilst also being able to identify the needs of individual pupils. Tracking progress is essential if teachers are to give classes, groups and individuals the support they need when it is needed most.

Thinking points

● Tracking is, in many cases, the culmination of a wide range of assessment procedures. Solid tracking gives colleagues the opportunity to stand back and review current attainment. It is in this format that teachers are able to identify trends, which can be used to review planning and pupil targets. In addition, it gives teachers solid evidence to request additional support. The longer schools use their tracking procedures the richer the evidence becomes.

● Teachers should review achievement and specifically look for children who plateau or who are not achieving as expected, based on prior attainment. This may be due to a variety of reasons, such as a new baby in the house or parents separating, but due consideration should be taken in order to evidence any dips or plateaus. These may also form the basis of a pupil review or parent consultation.

Tips, ideas and activities

● Creating assessment data can be time consuming, particularly pupil tracking. If your school has not done so already you should consider investing in an electronic assessment programme. These tools, detailed on page 42, can save hours of time. The time released can be spent engaging with the data and scrutinising it rather than simply creating it.

● The types of trend you should be looking for include:
  ○ Impacts on mobility on individual year groups.
  ○ Group trends such as minority groups or gender.
  ○ Patterns of achievement.
  ○ Children who are not achieving predicted results.
  ○ Attendance.

● Typically, most children achieve age-related standards, with fewer children achieving at high or low levels. On a graph this creates a bell curve. If this is not your finding then you should be ready to undertake an investigation so that you can rationalise this change in trend. This rationale should be reported within your school's Self Evaluation Form and may form a discussion within any future Ofsted inspection.

● Individual teachers must engage with their pupil tracking. Many schools link tracking, in some form, to performance management targets. This gives an appropriate incentive for it to remain prominent in the teacher's mind. Equally, it gives school leadership justification to devote training time to tracking.

● Tracking often reveals similar ability groups that would benefit from a shared intervention task. Over a period of time, you should be able to identify the impact that any intervention (such as a booster class) has on this group. Ideally, plot investment into the group – simply put, if there is no progress, then is the intervention in its current form working?

You Can... Moderate your assessments

Moderation is a key aspect of judgement making. Whether it is with your colleagues or external consultants, moderation is the filter that you can use to sharpen your skills when awarding a judgement. It ensures that everyone is, metaphorically, singing from the same hymn sheet. How you as a leader plan for moderation events and how regularly they take place depends on your school, the experience of staff and any specific school improvement plans.

Thinking points

● Experience grows as colleagues use a standard assessment programme, and with it you will build up a body of evidence. This evidence will have gone through enough scrutiny to accurately reflect a specific level judgement and can be used as moderation material when comparing current work. Equally, it can be meaningful material to use when training a colleague who is new to your moderation procedures, as it has been created through the school, not just as an external example from the Standards website.

● Moderation is an opportunity for colleagues to engage in a professional dialogue. This will fine-tune your skills, making the process a meaningful professional development opportunity as well as being a useful conversation about a child's standards.

● To maintain manageability, it is helpful to have a focus to your moderation procedures. The focus may reflect school improvement priorities, concerns or vary at each round.

Tips, ideas and activities

● If you are introducing a new assessment programme, such as Assessing Pupils' Progress (APP) or the Improving Schools Programme (ISP), moderation will have to form an element of your training programme. It is useful to set aside dedicated time, such as a twilight training session, for colleagues to handle example pieces of work that can be used to model the moderation process. Ideally an external consultant, such as a local authority representative, should be involved as they can present the national picture and fine-tune any moderation misunderstandings.

● Newly qualified teachers (NQTs), new colleagues and returning teachers may not be familiar with current assessment practices. A senior colleague, or yourself, can offer support by taking them through the assessment process and moderation procedures. This will ensure that they understand what to do whilst also maintaining a continuity of approach across the school.

● Knowing the practice in other schools can be a useful moderation tool in itself. If there is a school in your local network that has established good practice, it can be a practical resource for year group training (for example, Year 2 colleagues meeting) or for senior leaders to investigate.

● Currently, Reception and Years 2 and 6 require moderation training as part of end-of-key-stage assessments. Given that end-of-key-stage assessments are changing, it is wise to ensure that at least one member of each cohort attends appropriate training. Centralised training at your local Professional Development Centre should be advertised from April but, as changes to assessment procedures are not advertised until the autumn, it is worth regularly checking for training updates.

● In schools, moderation should be started as soon as assessments have been completed as the process will be fresh and give genuine meaning to the procedure.

You Can... Get the most from planned and impromptu observation

One of the core purposes of the Early Years is 'laying a secure foundation for future learning through learning and development that is planned around the individual needs and interests of the child, and informed by the use of ongoing observational assessment' (Statutory Framework for the Early Years Foundation Stage, 2008). It is from this core purpose that Early Years Practitioners (EYPs) across the country have developed creative and time-efficient observation strategies.

Thinking points

Observation, whether planned or impromptu, has always been a significant aspect of Early Years provision. In 2006 the *Early Years Foundation Stage Framework* stated that the:

'Early Years Foundation Stage (EYFS) requires those who plan and deliver early years provision to put children first; to listen to them and their parents; to observe what they can do; and to make them the most important influence on planning, observational assessment, routines and staffing'.

'It is important that practitioners ensure that they observe closely what children can do, and use those observations as the basis of assessment and planning of the next stages of children's development (there must be no tests for children at any stage of the EYFS)'.

Significantly this was then reiterated in the Statutory Framework for the Early Years Foundation Stage in 2008 almost word for word. It is the basis of all assessment and the conversations that should result from it.

Tips, ideas and activities

● Assessment must have a purpose and reflect the key areas of learning as stated in the Early Years Foundation Stage Profile.

● Ongoing observation of children participating in everyday activities is the most reliable way of building up an accurate picture of what children know, understand, feel, are interested in and can do. Practitioners should both plan observations and be ready to capture the spontaneous but important moments, such as discussion about snow falling or how they interact at an animal demonstration.

● All key adults should have a shared understanding about what to observe and how.

● Judgements of children's development and learning must be based on skills, knowledge, understanding and behaviour that are demonstrated consistently and independently.

● Effective assessment takes equal account of all aspects of the child's development and learning.

● Accurate assessment relies on contributions from a range of contexts, including both indoor and outdoor play. You may have a boy child who is reluctant to use a graphics table (even if a replica is placed outside). This requires some out-of-the box thinking, and clipboards by the sandpit or diggers may produce the early mark-making you require to complete an assessment.

● Assessments must actively engage parents in developing an accurate picture of the child's development.

● The Early Years Foundation Stage Statutory Framework 2008 can be accessed at www.standards.dcsf.gov.uk.

You Can... Get the most from a Learning Record

The Learning Record is a wonderful resource that, for many families, is a treasured book when returned home at the completion of Reception. It is a record of observations, conversations and home learning that is unique within the Primary setting. Parents/carers are particularly interested in their child's learning at this age and the Learning Record is a well-designed medium to capture this enthusiasm. Guided by Development Matters and the Early Learning Goals (formerly Stepping Stones), it is a powerful assessment tool that can accurately represent a child's progress.

Thinking points
● The Early Years Learning Record covers a child from birth to age five (the end of Reception). This long period of time will, no doubt, include changes in the child's learning environment. The aim of the Learning Record is to capture this important information. The success of this relies on three groups of people: the child, the parents/carers and the professionals involved. Under current guidance all three are invited to comment on their learning.

● Good continuity of learning can be achieved and children's progression is supported when a child joins a new setting that has systems in place to receive the Early Years Learning Record and continue parental involvement. Induction into the Foundation Stage and handover to Year 1 are two key transition periods where good continuity of the Learning Record can support best provision for children.

Tips, ideas and activities
● Focus-group observations lead into planning, which is led by Development Matters, which in turn produces the next steps (targets) for individual children/groups. This supports judgements made against the scale points that require moderation during the year (typically March), although some areas are adopting a cycle that includes three moderation visits a year (not necessarily per school) with the intention of identifying judgement gaps or strengths earlier rather than later.

● Indicate on the Learning Record if the observation is of a child- or adult-led activity. Date and initial all observations.

● Involving the parent is not only a requisite of the Learning Record, it is also the first important step in involving a parent with a child's complete learning journey. Share next steps with parents as often as you can. Parents can build on the focus at home as well.

● Talk to a child about their views and next steps. Capturing their comments and feelings is an important part of the Learning Record and will demonstrate development through the Early Years.

● Keep up to date with any changes in the child's circumstances, such as a new sibling, change of home, ill health or periods of absence. All these factors impact on a child's learning.

● Ensure that interests and areas of strong enthusiasm are regularly updated. It is normal for these to vary during a child's early years and it is important to keep a record of this.

● After the first term in Year 1, Learning Records should be returned to parents and families.

You Can... Successfully moderate in the Early Years

Moderation in the Early Years is an essential aspect of assessing professional judgments. The 117 scale points spread across six areas of learning makes this a potentially challenging task that requires good evidence. Inevitably, this demands a lot of professional time to document, assess, and assign scale-point judgements. There are also external demands from the local authority, which will moderate the process every other year in most cases. How you prepare for this will form thegreatest part of your discussion.

Thinking points

● Foundation Stage leads to Year 1 but at this point the National Curriculum, with its own set of standards, presents itself. These standards, although similar, are not necessarily harmonious, and currently a 9 roughly equates to a low level 1. However, many schools are extending the good practice of play-directed learning into Year 1, where a hybrid of Early Years scale-point assessment and National Curriculum assessment can work alongside each other depending on the needs of the child.

● You do not need to know all 117 scale points off by heart, as some moderators might suggest. Naturally, the more you use them, the more familiar you will be with them, and this will speed up your ability to assess against the scale points.

Tips, ideas and activities

● Be prepared. You will know in good time when your moderation meeting will take place. Generally you will be asked to present a selection of profiles although some authorities prefer to select their own (which means all your profiles will have to be fully up to date!)

● There a number of times during the year when you will need to have your paperwork and profiles up to date. Parent consultations are demanding but are also a useful motivator to get your records up to date. It is good practice to involve the children and parents/carers in contributing to observations and judgements. This can be done through home learning journals, which encourage parents to records special events, such as what they do during half-term holidays.

● Involve all adults who are working with your children in making observations. Your Early Years Practitioner (or Nursery Nurse) should be as capable as you at collecting evidence and equally qualified to challenge judgements.

● Collect a range of evidence about your children, including: spontaneous observations, focused observations, photographs, samples of work, narrative observations (over an extended period such as 20 minutes), videos or tape recordings. All of these should be annotated to show context support given.

● Take part in agreement trialling within your school and/or network to decide on the evidence and scale points to be given, using the support materials of the *Early Years Foundation Stage Profile Handbook*, CD-ROM of exemplification and the guidance provided from your local authority Early Years Support Service. Example profiles can be downloaded from the NAA website (www.naa.org.uk).

● After moderation, ensure that the next steps or points are addressed and shared with the headteacher.

You Can... Use IT to support Early Years assessment

IT has been used creatively in Early Years settings for many years. Indeed, photographing children at work was often the only way to provide evidence that they had met a specific learning goal, and is now generally standard practice in Reception and nursery classes. Today, a wide range of resources and tools are available that can support and fine-tune assessment procedures within the Early Years setting, while also utilising the good procedures already in place.

Thinking points

● The majority of occasions when people take photographs of children and young people are valid and do not provide any cause for concern. Unfortunately there are occasions when this is not the case and these are some of the risks associated with photographing children that must be taken into consideration:

  ○ The collection and passing on of images which may be misused.
  ○ The identification of individual children to facilitate abuse.
  ○ The identification of children in vulnerable circumstances.

● Typically, any Early Years photographing policy should take into account:

  ○ Obtaining the consent of the parent/carer.
  ○ That there is a legitimate purpose and reason for the photograph.
  ○ That the image is appropriate and does not capture the child during a non-public act such as going to the toilet;
  ○ That full names are not attached to photographs;
  ○ That you have an agreed display policy.
  ○ That use of mobile phone images is strictly monitored.

Tips, ideas and activities

● Digital cameras are an easy and useful resource. A low-priced camera will, today, produce acceptable image quality to evidence your objective. Printing images can be expensive but can be cheaper if you set your printer to black and white.

● A number of primary tracking programmes, such as Target Tracker, have Early Year equivalent programmes. Increasingly, these programmes are available on PDA hand-held devices that can be carried around and used to capture evidence immediately. The advantage of a digital record is that you can begin to sort any information immediately. As mobile devices, such as iPhones™, begin to deliver multiple mobile options with camera, database, tracking programme and note maker, we will begin to see more of them in classrooms as part of the suite of tools that teachers use to collect ongoing evidence for assessments.

● How schools store and protect photographs, particularly given the ease with which digital images can be distributed, should be considered. Increasingly, USB keys have some sort of encryption attached to them that can reduce the risk of distribution if the device is stolen.

● Flash USB keys, with their increasing memory capacity and reductions in price, are becoming the equivalent of a modern day laptop. Teachers now 'hot-seat' between computers using the Flash key as a portable hard-drive. This provides greater freedom for the individual teacher and is certainly preferable to lugging around a laptop, but the devices are very small and all too easy to lose. Backing up the device should be part of your weekly practice. Also, although hardwearing, occasional USB keys can be prone to corruption where, effectively, the key forgets the names of all your files and gives them a number instead. Finding any files is akin to looking for a needle in a haystack, so ensure you back up.

You Can... **Use IT to support assessment**

Colleagues in the Early Years will be well aware of the impact of digital cameras. The ability to immediately show a child a photograph you have taken of them at work affirms that what they are doing is worth photographing and must therefore be correct. It is a simple but effective form of assessment that has the bonus of improving that child's confidence. The immediacy that modern recording devices have can, arguably, have a dramatic impact on children's personal assessment. Unlike a teacher's ongoing assessments, which may or may not be shared with the child, IT can create a forum for sharing these assessments quickly and easily.

Thinking points

● Taking photographs, making videos and recording voices is a modern way of collecting evidence but requires a modern system to contain it. There is little point in collecting videos if you have no particular format for using them as a reliable piece of evidence. It is important, therefore, to consider why you are videoing the child, how the evidence is going to be stored (should this child have a virtual assessment folder?) and how it will be shared at a later date. This may include sharing with parents, colleagues and the child.

● There is little doubt that sharing a film of a child at work – such as performing a gym routine – is a powerful assessment tool for the child that they can use immediately. Given that most classrooms have data projectors it takes little effort to do this. So, modern digital technology can be used as part of ongoing assessments as well as in recording a finished product.

Tips, ideas and activities

● Digital cameras are a quick way of recording non-written assessments. Schools have generally invested in hardware, with each class having its own cameras, although even budget mobile phones have passable cameras on them. For the purposes of assessment, the image does not need to be perfect. most modern computers have Bluetooth® chips included, making it relatively easy to download an image. If you are considering printing the image for an assessment folder, a black and white photograph will generally suffice. You may want to change the printer settings as it may automatically print at a higher specification if it recognises the image as a photograph, which would use a lot of ink.

● Handheld voice recorders, often shaped to look like a microphone, are cheap and easy to use. Given that there is renewed emphasis on speaking and listening, the ability to record these opportunities is becoming increasingly important. A growing number of recorders are available with USB connections, so that they can be inserted directly into a computer or laptop without an additional cable. These tools are useful for recording poetry, music, singing and voiceovers, which can be used with another computer program, such as PowerPoint®.

● Mini, mobile-phone sized video-recorders have now fallen below £100. Kodak's Zi6 and Flip Video's Mino both offer compact, high definition (albeit at the low end of high definition) recorders with flip USB connection so, like the microphones, they can download straight to your computer. They have limited functionality but because they are so small and easy to use they can readily record assessments, such as PE or a group of musicians, in a way that a camera cannot.

You Can... **Use the internet to assess**

Less than ten years ago we would have marvelled at what the internet could offer. Today it is an accepted form of communication which, for many teachers, has become their first reference point. Indeed, many organisations are so aware of this that they publish straight to the web rather than printing documents. The advantage of this is that there is an archive of resources within easy access. This includes a wealth of assessment materials, training videos and presentations from around the world.

Thinking points

● Websites are still in the process of evolving. Although many are beginning to stabilise, it is still possible that a site you had previously used for assessment either no longer exists or has been updated to the point that it is difficult to find what you now need. As the technology for web-design is still developing at a great pace (think of websites from ten years ago compared to current ones), it is very tempting for the web designer to totally redevelop a site to keep up with current trends.

● Pupil trackers, such as Target Tracker (see page 56) are moving online. This is currently the practice in secondary schools. By 2011, all primary schools must be able to communicate with parents electronically and this will include assessments. Online tools will make this easier for the parent and the teacher.

Tips, ideas and activities

● The National Curriculum in Action website has a wealth of pupil assessments that can be used for moderation purposes. These range from scanned examples of genuine levelled written work to mini films of children performing an activity such as gymnastics. Each assessment is accompanied with a commentary that includes an activity description and objectives, an appropriate example of a resource (this can take the form of a scanned image, piece of audio or film clip) and notes about the entry. To access this resource go to curriculum. qca.org.uk/key-stages-1-and-2/assessment/nc-in-action/index. aspx

● The National Foundation for Educational Research (NFER) has produced a dozen downloadable assessment leaflets. They cover most aspects of assessment, including how to communicate with parents. They are available at www.nfer. ac.uk (go to the 'Research areas' tab and then click on 'Assessment').

● Teachers TV (www.teachers.tv) contains dozens of 15-minute films on assessment. Each film generally has a suite of additional resources attached to it so that you can practise the aspect discussed on the film. The site has a good search engine and will generally find quite specific films, such as pupil conferences.

● Google™ has recently updated its search engine to include video and scholar searches. Searching for Assessment for Learning will now create a standard website list as well as give the options for a range of videos and scholastic texts. Use 'Assessment for Learning' as an example search to see the range of resources available.

● Certain sites are more prone to change than others. For example government-sponsored sites are influenced by the governing party and by changes in strategy. In these cases expect the site to significantly change in style when the party or strategy does. Unfortunately these tend to be the sites we use most often!

You Can... Create useful data from your assessments

Tracking pupil progress, particularly if you are an ISP-intensive school, used to be an arduous task of cutting and pasting across documents. Using IT can speed up this process and allow you to move from an administrative role to an evaluative role, in which you are engaging with the data rather than just inputting numbers. This change is important as it releases time to focus on individual pupils and to track their attainment across the year.

Thinking points

● Most teachers are comfortable with using programs such as Microsoft Word® or PowerPoint®. Excel, on the other hand, can feel alien as numbers and formula drive it. Excel is, however, simply a number cruncher and most programs that use it (be it an assessment tracker or a budget sheet) will use it in its simplest form. If you make a mistake it has, like Word, an 'undo' button that can be used to correct any errors. There are plenty of online tutorials available (search for 'Excel training') or ask a colleague. It is an important program and you will have to understand how it works.

● Mobility, particularly in inner-city schools, can be a challenging issue. Whatever programs you use, you should aim to track the number of children who have left and entered your cohort (year group) during the year so that mobility can be monitored and its impact on attainment evaluated.

Tips, ideas and activities

● When a child leaves your class, your programme should be able to project what their end-of-key-stage level would have been. This type of information is important when assessing the school's value added score.

● As well as grouping ability within the class, your data should reveal the type of progress any individual child has made. If a child has reached a plateau or regressed you should have a rationale as to why this happened or have implemented strategies to support the child. It should not be satisfactory to accept that a child is on-track if they are at an age-appropriate level when their earlier education demonstrated they were achieving above age-appropriate levels.

● Data is powerful but can also be misleading, particularly when associated with small numbers of children. You might be tracking a particular ethnic group and notice that only 66 per cent has achieved age-appropriate levels. The reality is that it might be only one child out of three who has not reached their target.

● It is possible to create a wide range of charts, tables and graphs that can look very professional but to the untrained eye are confusing. It is better to keep to simple charts as they will convey a clearer message when talking to non-professionals.

● Computer-generated data can be easy to transfer to colleagues in the form of an attachment. Most email browsers will allow you to do this. If you are using the latest version of any software it is best to save your document as an older version as your colleague may not have the latest edition and might struggle to open the document.

You Can... **Use data for predictions**

The longer a school collects data on individual children the more powerful the data becomes. Plateaus, learning leaps and other trends can be tracked, all of which go towards creating a picture of any one child's learning journey through primary education. The more you interact with the data the better you will be at reading it and the faster you will become at recognising where a standard trend is diverged from by a particular child. Why these changes occur, and what expectations are reasonable, can be addressed if you have a secure knowledge of where their predicted learning should be.

Thinking points

● When children have hit plateaus or are simply coasting at a slightly lower level than expected, teachers should ask why. There could be any number of reasons, such as change to class dynamics or friendship circles, a new sibling, moving house, parental separation or bereavement. These are tangible reasons that can explain dips in expected learning. If there is no organic rationale, then a re-grading might be considered if the trend is persistent.

● Tracking programmes, such as those discussed on page 56, are extremely useful tools that can potentially save hours of time. Diagnostic charts and tables are useful pieces of data for tracking results but are time consuming to create. If your school does not yet have any tracking software, it could be argued that you are not engaging with each child's tracking to the degree now expected by Ofsted and parents.

Tips, ideas and activities

● Typically, a child progresses two thirds of a level in an academic year. This is relatively straightforward to track from the assessments at the end of Year 2 by adding approximately two-thirds of a level to each year group (other than in Year 3 when a transition impact generally creates a dip in learning and children typically move by one-third of a level). Even without computer-aided support, schools should be able to track predicted end-of-year standards for each child by adding the following amount of sub-levels: Y3 – one sub-level, Y4–6 – two sub-levels each. Usually, a child who achieves 2b at the end of Key Stage 1 should be attaining a solid level 4 by the end of Year 6.

● Predicting results for Years 1 and 2 from Reception is more of a challenge, as the Early Years goals do not currently match the National Curriculum. That said, a child who is attaining a P9 at the end of Foundation Stage can be loosely translated as working at 1c and would therefore be predicted to achieve a level 3 at the end of KS1 and level 5 at the end of KS2.

● Predictions are only a benchmark. It goes without saying that children do not learn at the same rate and that peaks, troughs and plateaus are normal. However, having this benchmark allows teachers to engage with the data using a fixed reference point on expected learning. This can form a rationale for learning interventions or discussions with parents.

● Children can learn at accelerated rates. This is most evident in Year 6 when children can, for any number of reasons not necessarily related to planned intervention, defy the odds and achieve results way beyond predictions. This is always a wonderful bonus and acts as a useful reminder that predicted results can sometimes be wildly wrong!

You Can... Choose the best assessment tool to fit your class

In today's media-rich classrooms, filled with interactive whiteboards, laptops, palm readers, media players and other tools, it seems natural to use the opportunities that IT programs have to offer for assessment. The range of tools appearing on the market include digital formal assessments, tools to track standards and online resources that can support moderation, which are particularly useful with subjects such as PE for which you might not have many examples. Added to this are learning platforms that will also include an assessment section that parents can access. The issue facing modern teachers is how to efficiently get the most out of the many resources that are available.

Thinking points

● In the last five years, schools have begun to utilise IT to streamline assessment procedures. With the growing range of resources available, it is easy to be seduced by what the programs can do rather than what you are looking for. There is little doubt that IT saves time and can manipulate data quickly. With the growing number of laptops in classrooms it is likely that we will see an end to paper-based assessments in the not-so-distant future. That said, it is important to keep at the forefront what it is you are assessing and why, not what the program wants you to assess.

● Formal test-based assessments have been available as programs for several years. They have the advantage of marking and evaluating the work on your behalf. The role of the teacher, in this case, moves from 'administrative-marker' to 'professional-assessor', freeing your time to scrutinise the results.

Tips, ideas and activities

Don't be intimidated by some of the larger programs. If you are looking for one aspect, such as highlighting if a child is on track, then learn how to use that function and build from it. It is likely that programs in the future will become easier to access as publishers become familiar with what teachers want.

● Schools will have access to RAISEonline (Reporting and Analysis for Improvement through School Self-Evaluation), an online government assessment tool. This program provides data created from the Key Stage 1 and 2 tests. Its aim is to enable schools to share a common assessment programme that allows the user to observe value-added trends and contextual information about the school and targets, and also provides an opportunity to edit and manage individual pupil data. It has much potential but has had a few teething problems.

● There is a range of tracking programmes available on the open market:
  ○ Target Tracker (www.targettracker.org) does as the name suggests and tracks children's standards as they progress from year to year. This can be managed either termly or half-termly. Once an individual's data has been inputted, the program will make any calculations on your behalf, including progression within the class, groups or cohort. The programme is based on Excel and will perform any of the standard sorting functions that you would expect with an Excel document.
  ○ Targ*SATS* (www.targsats.com) is a similar program, also based on Excel, which will create any number of charts and tables once it has been populated with data. Like Target Tracker, it can produce next-steps targets and will highlight its termly data to reflect schools that are using the Intensive Support Programme (ISP) codes.

Teaching Assistant communication sheet

Communication with other adults

Name of adult:

Date:

Class:

Name of teacher:

Time of lesson:

Curriculum area:

Lesson objective:

Children in focus group:

Key questions:

Lesson brief:

Notes on children's progress:

Assessment:

Additional comments

Tracking sheet

Class:

Focus group:

Assessment area:

NC Level	Summer (previous year)				Autumn				Spring				Summer				NC Level
5+																	5+
4a																	4a
4b																	4b
4c																	4c
3a																	3a
3b																	3b
3c																	3c
2a																	2a
2b																	2b
2c																	2c
1a																	1a
1b																	1b
1c																	1c
Below Level 1																	Below Level 1

The table below shows the national average entry levels and expected levels of attaining for each year group. These can be plotted on the grid above so that a focus group can be tracked during the year. For impacts on learning to be measurable, track back to either end of KS1 or Foundation Stage Profiles for end-of-phase attainment levels. If a child was a 9 at the end of Foundation Stage you would expect them to achieve l3 by Y2, moving to l5 by the end of Y6.

Year	Entry level	Expected level
Y1	1c	1b/1a
Y2	1a/2c	2b/2a
Y3	2c/2b	2a/3c
Y4	2a/3c	3b/3a
Y5	3c/3b	3a/4c
Y6	3a/4c	4b/4a

Ongoing observation

Class:
Child:

Adults involved with child's learning:
Date of birth: Season:

Date	Lesson objective	Comments	Action from observation

Learning journey

Subject

Date:

I can target:

I can target:

I can target:

I can target:

Steps to success...

Steps towards the target:
l. in poetry and narrative. Make inferences based on evidence from texts: making reference to the themes, language used and viewpoint.

Steps towards the target:

Steps towards the target:

Steps towards the target:

Bibliography

Assessment for Learning: Putting it into Practice by Paul Black (Open University Press, 2003)

Assessment for Learning: Putting it into Practice, by Black, Harrison & Lee (Open University Press, 2003)

Active Learning Through Formative Assessment by Shirley Clarke (Hodder Education, 2008)

Enriching Feedback in the Primary Classroom by Shirley Clarke (Hodder & Stoughton, 2003)

Assessment and Learning: Theory, Policy and Practice by John Gardner (Sage Press, 2006)

Making Formative Assessment Work: Effective Practice in the Primary Classroom by Hall and Burke (Open University Press, 2004)

Questioning in the Primary School (Successful Teaching) by Wragg & Brown (Routledge, 2001)

Explaining in the Primary School (Successful Teaching) by Wragg & Brown (Routledge, 2001)

Talking, Listening and Learning: Effective Talk in the Primary Classroom by Myhill, Jones & Hopper (Open University Press, 2005)

Exploring Talk in School: Inspired by the Work of Douglas Barnes by Mercer & Hodgkinson (SAGE Publications, 2008)

Useful websites

Assessment:
- www.teachers.tv – search for 'assessment'
- www.nfer.ac.uk – includes a series of useful leaflets about assessment
- www.nationalstrategies.standards.dcsf.gov.uk/primary/assessment
- www.everychildmatters.gov.uk

Assessment for Learning:
- www.assessment4learning.co.uk
- www.qca.org.uk/qca_4336.aspx – directs you to the QCA website that defines the AfL guiding principles

Foundation Stage Profile:
- www.standards.dfes.gov.uk/eyfs/resources/downloads/eyfs_handbook_web.pdf – for a copy of the handbook
- www.standards.dfes.gov.uk/eyfs/site/profile/index.htm – the Standards website

Improving Schools Programme:
- www.nationalstrategies.standards.dcsf.gov.uk/node/85089 – for a full document download
- www.edu.dudley.gov.uk/primary/pdm/introducingtheisp.pdf – a useful booklet designed by Dudley LA

Assessing Pupils' Progress:
- http://nationalstrategies.standards.dcsf.gov.uk/primary/primaryframework/assessment/app – the standards core APP website
- www.nationalstrategies.standards.dcsf.gov.uk/node/158443 – a useful brief about APP
- www.nationalstrategies.standards.dcsf.gov.uk/node/160703 – directs you to a useful document

All websites accessed June 2009.

Index

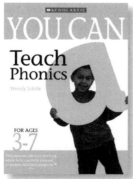

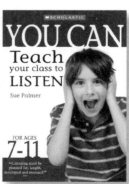